50p

Pamela Westland, a jo........ was formerly editor of Now a top freelance, crafts, a book on home pressing flowers and flo several other highly succ *The Everyday Gourmet, B* available as Granada

Pamela Westland is now a confirmed rustic and lives in a fourteenth-century farmhouse in Wethersfield, Essex.

By the same author

A Taste of the Country
The Everyday Gourmet
Bean Feast
One-pot Cooking
The Yoghurt Cookbook
The Encyclopedia of Spices
The 60-minute Cookbook
Food For Keeps
The High-Fibre Cookbook

PAMELA WESTLAND

The Complete Grill Cookbook

GRANADA

London Toronto Sydney New York

Published by Granada Publishing Limited in 1983

ISBN 0 586 05773 0

A Granada Paperback Original
Copyright © Pamela Westland 1983

Granada Publishing Limited
Frogmore, St Albans, Herts AL2 2NF
and
36 Golden Square, London W1R 4AH
515 Madison Avenue, New York, NY 10022, USA
117 York Street, Sydney, NSW 2000, Australia
60 International Boulevard, Rexdale, Ontario, R9W 6J2, Canada
61 Beach Road, Auckland, New Zealand

Printed and bound in Great Britain by
Cox & Wyman Ltd, Reading
Set in Times

Granada ®
Granada Publishing ®

CONTENTS

Measurements and Quantities

Please follow either the metric or the Imperial measurements for each recipe. The amounts are not accurately converted, but 'rounded up', and so are not successfully inter-changeable.

All recipes throughout the book serve four people, unless otherwise stated.

Introduction

It's impossible to believe how versatile a contact grill can be, or what an amazing range of snacks and treats you can produce on a sandwich maker, until you yourself have cooked on one.

I started work on this book 'cold', never having cooked on either appliance before, full of enthusiasm for a new project; completely open-minded about the possibilities, and slightly apprehensive about finding enough variety to fill a book.

I needn't have worried. After only a few weeks of testing, my problem was clearly going to be not which recipes to put in, but which of the hundreds I devised, adapted from conventional methods and tested I could bear to leave out. And so I have a filing basket piled high and toppling with ideas that worked perfectly on a table-top grill, were absolutely delicious, but didn't quite make the grade!

However enthusiastic you are to get started on the enjoyment of cooking and eating, do please take time to read the first two chapters, on getting to know your appliance and making the most of its potential. You will find lots of little tips, hints and thoughts almost in note form as they occurred to me; they might prove food for thought for you, too.

And as you dip into the recipes and read the numerous alternative suggestions I have added for good measure, I hope your confidence will grow and you will become more and more adventurous. It won't be long before you can expertly go through other cookery books on your shelves, make a quick mental adaptation in the method and ask yourself, Why on earth do I need an oven?

1 Getting to Know Your Appliance

There's no doubt about it, once you start using a contact grill or its smaller brother, the sandwich maker, you'll wonder how you ever managed without one. As you can see from the extremely wide variety of recipes in this book, for starters, main dishes, sweets and puddings, as well as baking of all kinds, the versatility of the modern contact grill makes it one of the most indispensable pieces of cooking equipment available. When it comes to the compact sandwich maker, there's no limit to the possibilities and no end to the permutations of savoury or sweet fillings. Only one's own imagination can limit the usefulness of this little appliance.

Add to this the speed with which the appliances can provide you with appetizing, piping hot meals or toasted sandwiches and snacks, plus the relatively low energy costs compared with those of full-size conventional cookers, and you will understand why I believe that either, or better still both, of these appliances should always be close at hand in any self-respecting kitchen or bed-sit.

For years, grilling has been regarded as one of the quickest methods of cooking and one which food specialists and professional chefs alike agree retains the maximum possible nutrients and flavour of the food. And now doctors are convinced that we need a higher proportion of fibre in our diet to ensure continuing good health. This means that bread, especially wholemeal bread, is given official blessing as a beneficial and necessary part of our diet. So toasted sandwiches, with relatively low-fat fillings, can be one of the healthiest hot snack foods around.

Contact grills, of course, are capable of producing a whole lot more than just tasty, succulent grills. By using a tailor-made baking dish, usually supplied with the appliance, you can explore a large range of close encounters of another kind. In effect, this means that not only all the foods that can be cooked on a conventional grill, but also a very high proportion of those that can be cooked in a conventional oven can now be handled by a standard-size contact grill — subject to the number of hungry mouths you have to feed.

The 'power house' of both appliances is the two cast aluminium heating plates which transfer a rapid and evenly-spread heat to the food. The actual cooking process is so rapid because the heat is concentrated on the food both by conduction and the penetration of what is usually (though not correctly) termed infra-red heat.

The plates of both contact grills and sandwich makers are coated with a non-stick material, such as Teflon: a blessing when, as inevitably happens, cheese, jam or other sticky fillings ooze on to the heated surface.

The personality of the various brands of sandwich maker is most evident in the different moulded patterns used for the plates — shells, scallops, ridged bars, whirled circles or what-ever. Some sandwich makers have sharp cutting edges through the centre of the plates and so what goes into the appliance as a single and rather large sandwich comes out as a pair of much more dainty portions, the filling neatly and firmly sealed in all round.

On all makes of contact grill, both the upper and lower heating plates are ribbed on one side, on their contact sur-faces. This ribbing not only gives an attractive 'grilled look', but also quickly seals the food that is in direct contact, and allows the heat to radiate backwards and forwards between the plates to ensure rapid and thorough cooking. On some models, the grill plates are reversible, offering flat, smooth 'other' sides for griddling — and a whole new range of cooking possibilities.

Contact grill cooking is healthy cooking. Because of the efficient non-stick finish on the plates, you need very little if any extra fat when grilling. The calorie-laden animal fats are also expelled from meats and fish and channelled away. Most contact grills have special drainage channels at the corners of both top and bottom plates, and some manufacturers supply a drip tray with the appliance. If yours does not have one, be sure to place a suitable receptacle in position before you start cooking fatty foods — the overspill can make a sorry mess of your working surfaces.

Conditioning your appliance

Before using your contact grill or sandwich maker for the first time, you must 'condition' the non-stick coated plates. Brush them with a little cooking oil or margarine, switch on the appliance and heat it in the open position for about 5 minutes. Switch off the appliance, leave it to cool, then wipe off any surplus oil with kitchen paper. Your contact grill or sandwich toaster is now ready to use.

Indicator lights

You should always pre-heat your contact grill or sandwich toaster before use. Some models have two lights, one to show when the appliance is switched on, and a second one to indicate when the cooking temperature is reached. If yours does not have a 'power on' light, you can fit a 13-amp safety plug that incorporates one, so you can see at a glance when the appliance is connected to the power. During the cooking process the indicator light may go on and off from time to time. This is quite normal and shows that the thermostatic temperature control is functioning and maintaining correct cooking temperature — whether or not your appliance has variable heat settings. If your contact grill provides a range of heat settings from High to Low, you can alter the setting during cooking without switching off the appliance.

Cooking times

As I point out in other chapters, the cooking times given throughout the book are as accurate as I could make them, given the range of power ratings of the various appliances. You may need to vary them slightly to suit your particular appliance and your own personal preferences — readers who enjoy their steak really rare will naturally cook it for a much shorter time than those who like it cooked to a frazzle.

Equally, it has not been possible to be specific about the heat settings for each different contact grill model. Some appliances use a 'Low, Medium, High' rating, some use a 1 to 3 scale, and another gives a variable of 1 through to 5. I have used the terms Low, Medium and High throughout the recipes, and it should be easy to relate Low to the setting numbered 1, Medium to 2 or 3, and High to either 4 or 5 on your dial.

In all matters of timing the main thing to remember is that this means of cooking is fast and when both sides of the food are in close contact with the grill plates, it is nearly *twice as fast*. It is better to be safe, by having an occasional peep just before the recommended time is up, than sorry that you didn't.

Cooking positions

Sandwich makers are always used with the top and bottom cooking plates closed together, the sandwich or snack touch-ing — in close contact with — both of them. The bread, pastry or other casing will cook to a delicious golden toastiness *only* if it is in close contact and so it is important to fill the sandwiches, pasties and pies generously enough for this to happen.

Contact grills offer a wide range of cooking positions. First, there is the close contact one, when both top and bottom plates touch the food in question, whether it is a steak, chop, whole fish or a sandwich. The upper section of the appliance is lightly sprung so that the top rests gently on the food and does not flatten it unduly. However, for more delicate food items — rolled fillets of fish, or stuffed green peppers, for example — it is better to place them directly on to the lower plate with the upper one in what one manufacturer calls the 'grill and toast' position — parallel to the lower one but suspended above the food. This is the position to choose, too, for toasted open sandwiches, caramelizing the tops of baked custards and browning meringue toppings.

Still in this suspended position, the hotplate can be lowered over the baking dish. This is when the appliance thinks it's an oven. The baking dish becomes a baking sheet for pastries, biscuits, buns and cakes; it becomes a gratin dish for baked vegetables, moussaka, lasagne and so on; a pie dish for single- or double-crust savoury or fruit pies, and, with an improvised lid of cooking foil it turns into a highly efficient casserole. You can also use the baking dish to reheat foods in a trice — from complete one-dish meals to a couple of bread rolls — and to thaw frozen foods. A word about this versatile baking dish. If the one that comes with your appliance does not have a non-stick finish, or if it has a ridged and wavy base, do invest in a flat-bottomed non-stick version as your personal extra. It will more than repay the cost.

To toast just one side, you can cook on the lower hotplate alone, with the upper one locked in the vertical position at 90 degrees to the horizontal one. Do remember, though, that the vertical plate is still being heated to the same temperature as the horizontal one — so mind your fingers!

Then there is the opened-out-flat position, with both grill plates horizontal. This way you have double the space and is specially useful for models with flat, smooth sides for griddling — you can cook a whole batch of drop scones or biscuits at one go. This way the appliance can be turned into a useful hotplate: an extra hostess aid, to keep casseroles, vegetable dishes and crockery warm before a meal. Use the lowest heat setting for cooking or tableware that is not specially heat-resistant, and don't put dishes straight from the refrigerator on it.

One model of snack maker offers even more versatility, with four sets of removable plates to toast sandwiches, make waffles, wafers and perfectly shaped hamburgers. The plates are quick and easy to change and insert and give you the facility of producing a varied three-course meal in moments — cheese wafers with soup for the first course, say; hamburgers for the centre of attention; and crisp, crunchy waffles oozing with soft fruits and soured cream for a spectacular finale.

Care and maintenance

As you will know from using non-stick frying-pans, these protective coatings are precious. When turning cooked food, stirring food in the baking dish or serving, use only wooden or tough plastic spatulas, fish slices or spoons.

All the appliances are easy-care and low on maintenance — the non-stick finishes see to that. As soon as you have finished cooking, switch off and unplug the appliance and leave it in the open (L-shaped) position to cool. Never leave a hot appliance opened out flat — think what a danger it could be to children, cats or visitors. When the cooking plates are still slightly warm, wipe them over with a clean, damp cloth. Never allow the heating elements to become wet and *never*,

never dunk the appliance in water. If any food has spilled and solidified or burnt on the plates, brush them with a little cooking oil, leave it for a few minutes, then wipe it away. Never use scouring powders, metal tools, knives or anything abrasive to clean the plates; there's just no need.

Allow removable cooking plates to cool before washing them. Immersing very hot plates in water could cause them to warp. Wash them in hot soapy water or detergent, using a cloth or soft brush and *no* scouring pads.

Check list

Careful reading of the manufacturer's instructions will guide you in the use of your appliance. Here is a short check list of safeguards:

- Read all the maker's instructions before using.
- Do not touch the outer casing when in use. Always use the handles.
- Never leave the appliance unattended when there are children (or hungry pets) around.
- Make sure the flex does not hang over the edge of working surface or table.
- Don't use the appliance on surfaces which can be damaged by heat, or near a hot cooker plate, gas ring or close to a hot oven.
- Do not use your appliance in very confined spaces. There should be sufficient space above and on all sides to permit adequate circulation of air.
- Always switch off the appliance and remove the plug (fused, 13 amp) from the mains immediately after use.
- To save space many appliances may be stored away in the upright position. Before storing ensure that all plates are fully locked and handle clips are in position.

Manufacturers

Here is a list of the leading manufacturers of contact grills and sandwich makers. You will find their full addresses on page 229. As makers introduce new and improved models the specification details given here are, of course, subject to change, as are the actual model numbers and names.

Happily you can now buy contact grills and sandwich makers at virtually all the shops that sell other domestic electrical appliances — and that includes Electricity Board showrooms, specialist electrical goods shops, department stores and some kitchen equipment shops. Wherever you buy your new appliance make sure that, in addition to the instruction and recipe booklet, it comes with a full guarantee for a year's use.

CONTACT GRILLS

Model	*Rating Watts	Pre-set Thermostat	Variable Heat Control	Detachable Plates	Reversible Plates	Baking Dish Supplied	180 Degree Opening
Moulinex Express Cooker & Combination Grill	1600	●		●		●	
Rima Cooking Centre 904	2000	●	●	●		●	●
Rima Cooking Centre 903	2000	●	●	●	●	●	●
Rima Cooking Centre 902	1400	●		●	●	●	●
Rima Grill 900	1200	●				●	
Sunbeam Fast Food Centre GR55	2000		●	●	●	●	●

*Power Supply: All 240 volts A.C., unless otherwise stated

SANDWICH MAKERS

Model	Rating (watts)	Pre-set thermostat	Variable heat control	Number of sandwiches
Breville 8-Up Snackmaker	1700	●		4
Breville Snack 'n' Sandwich Toaster SG3	900	●		2
Kenwood Sandwich Toaster, A104	1550	●	*	4
Kenwood Sandwich Toaster, A 103	830	●	*	2
Kenwood Toasted Sandwich Maker, A102	600	●		2
Pifco Sandwich Toaster	700	*		2
Rima Party Sandwich Centre, 936	1750	*		6

	Watts		Number
Rima Snack 'n' Toasted Sandwich Centre, 935	1200		2
Rima Sandwich Toaster	700	*	2
Sunbeam GR 10	1440	*	4
Sunbeam GR 11	800	*	2
Sunbeam GR 31	800	*	2
Tefal Super Snack* (with detachable Sandwich and Hamburger plates)	1000	*	2
Tefal Sandwich Maker**	1000	*	2
Tower Sandwich Toaster	1000	*	2

*Sets of Waffle and Grill Plates available

**Sets of Grill, Waffle and Wafer Plates available

Power Supply: All 240 volts A.C., unless otherwise stated

2 Making the Most of Your Appliance

For a one-pot dish cooked in minutes instead of hours; for cook-and-come-again party desserts; lazy, leisurely evenings in the garden or on the balcony; showmanship dishes produced at the table with a fine flourish; for days when it's too hot to light the oven; if you live in a bed-sitter, share a kitchen or have a holiday home, a contact grill is the perfect answer, with a sandwich maker not very far behind.

Contact grill

Let's take the more versatile appliance first. Once you have cooked single- or double-crust meat pies, moussaka, baked cheesecake, chocolate pudding and a batch of bread and cakes on a contact grill, you really do begin to wonder if you ever need an oven. Perhaps you could hire one just to cook the Christmas turkey!

Indeed, the appliance has many positive advantages over any oven I've ever used. First and foremost, of course, it cuts down considerably on cooking time. To make a meat pie, for instance, you fry the vegetables and meat in the baking dish between the grill plates first, then simply rest the pastry on top, lower the top grill again, and in a quarter of an hour the meal is on the table. Look up a standard recipe for *Baklava* for example, and you might decide you haven't the time — something like 1½ hours — to make it. Look up my recipe for this wickedly sticky honey and nut pastry, and you will find it's cooked in a trice — in 10 minutes, to be precise.

Fuel saving is one of its great bonuses. In many of the main-dish recipes you would need to light a hotplate to pre-fry the ingredients, the oven to bake it and probably the grill to crisp up a last-minute topping. Now it's all done in one continuous operation.

I've always been dreadfully mean about using fuel and oven heat, long before we all realized that 'Save It' was a national duty and not just a personal expedient. I have never lit the oven just to make a single batch of scones or cook jacket potatoes; it seems immoral. So when I've run out of time to make full use of the oven (whip up something else to cook at the same temperature) I've gone without, rather than waste it.

Now, with the table-top cooker and the pared-down timing, one-off dishes no longer seem an extravagance. Even so, it's a challenge, and one that's easily met, to plan several dishes around the contact grill once it's switched on.

While the grill is heating up — and you should always have it pre-heated before you start cooking — there is a chance to put a small pan on the lower grill plate to melt butter or honey for the start of a flapjack recipe maybe or to make a sauce or even to heat stock. Always look out for this possibility before you light a hotplate almost as a reflex action, and pour fuel costs down the drain.

Still on economy, when the contact grill is closed for cooking, I make use of the top surface to heat soup bowls or plates, or to keep part of the meal warm, a sauce perhaps or the rice. But do be careful: never pile up the appliance, pyramid fashion, if there are young children or fleet-footed cats about. An accident could cost more than you save.

With cooking time so speedy, even a small contact grill can play a big part in a party. You can have batches of pitta bread wrapped in foil on top, cook a succession of meat or fish kebabs as fast almost as you can serve them, and have scrumptious party pastries ready to follow on.

Talking of entertaining, contact grills have a number of very special social graces. If you are entertaining single-handed (always a problem: do you leave your guests alone, or ask them to follow you into the kitchen while you stir and brush and glaze?) bring the appliance into the dining room and you can relax, enjoy their company and be confident that the food can't spoil while your back is turned. This is the occasion for foil-wrapped parcels of fish or meat and vegetables, complete little meals in themselves, beautifully cooked with no lingering smell; out they come, ready to serve, in goes a dish of spiced fruit or a crumble, and home go your guests full of praise and wonderment.

When it's too hot to light the oven, the contact grill comes into its own. When it's too hot even to cook indoors, all you need is a socket outlet near a door or window, an extension lead and you can produce alfresco meals, if not exactly barbecues, in the garden or on the balcony. Grilled steak or escallopes with that inviting criss-cross pattern the professionals achieve, honey-glazed chops, jacket potatoes with help-yourself fillings, or pancakes to roll up around a selection of sweet or savoury sauces: your contact grill can help you create an air of relaxed informality.

The contact grill is nothing if not versatile; if you don't have the whole of the great outdoors at your disposal, but the slightly more restricting limits of a bedsitter, a shared kitchen or a holiday home, it will be your faithful right-hand. It sits on a table-top, packs away in no more than the space of a decent dictionary, and takes the whole flurry out of cooking. If you're not in your own home, it's definitely a case of preferring to cook on the devil (or angel?) you know, than on an unknown and maybe temperamental stranger.

What exactly your contact grill will mean to you, I can't say. We all have our strong and our weak points. I've never been very good at pastry or cakes and have been surprised, more than just pleased, if something I made turned out really well. See how you get on. But honestly, since I have been cooking on a contact grill, I've never known results like it. The best choux, shortcrust and puff pastry I've ever made have been on what I now call the 'magic machine'; the lightest Victoria sponge and the crispiest biscuits and flapjacks, too. Somehow, with the little cooker there before your eyes, and with progress-checking made so easy (no disastrous flops as you open the oven door) failures just seem out of the question.

Once you have a contact grill that makes cooking so quick, easy and almost foolproof, there could well be less incentive to batch-bake for the freezer: the time you save is so very much less now. But when you do want to defrost frozen food, that's quicker too. If, for example, you freeze a gratinated dish or a curry in the baking dish, turn it out when it's frozen and seal and label it: all you have to do is to turn it back into the baking dish, pop it in the grill and reheat it. No fussing about checking the size of dishes, and no time and fuel wasted. Bread, rolls, cakes, pastries, all defrost in moments between the directional and very close heat of the two grill plates.

Sandwich maker

No wonder many manufacturers have searched around for names that are more all-encompassing than simply 'sandwich maker', for the range of things you can cook on one of these snappy little appliances defies the imagination, too. Sandwiches with white, brown, black, speckled and any other type of bread you care to mention goes without saying. But it makes the most amazing pastries, too, sealing in the filling so that (always assuming you haven't left a gaping hole in the paste) it positively never oozes out; meat pies with minced meat or home-made or even canned pie fillings come into the main-meal class, little Greek cheese and herb pies come into the party section. For, quick and easy as they are to make, you could make a whole batch – lots of different fillings to add to the variety — and have them ready in the fridge or freezer to just keep on coming. Choux, shortcrust, puff pastry, pizza dough, scones and bread, they all cook like a dream in the sandwich maker and offer a whole range of main dishes, snacks and tea-time treats. If you're new to the appliance, I think the recipes in Chapter Eight will astound you.

But usefulness doesn't stop here. Vegetable pasties toasted to a golden brown — potato and parsnip cakes frizzled to a deep toffee colour, for example — make perfect accompaniments, or scrummy snacks in their own right. And what about the hot vegetables to go with all those little savoury pies? No problem. Brush the sandwich plates generously with butter, pop a pasty in one side and a few sliced cooked potatoes and raw mushrooms in the other, and you have a complete meal on a plate. Bubble and squeak, that old English favourite, of cooked potatoes and Brussels sprouts or cabbage, sliced potatoes layered with onion rings, they all turn out toasty-tasty.

If there is one slight problem, it's visual. If your sandwich maker has two or four plates with a similar shape, then whatever you make turns out looking the same — ridged, scalloped or whatever. You could perfectly well serve whole meals made on the appliance. Let's see, cheese and herb soda bread with a soup or a dip for the first course; tuna-fish patties with sauté potatoes and sliced mushrooms for the entrée, and blueberry choux puffs for dessert. The only trouble is, with everything coming up roses, so to speak, you're going to get heartily sick of the shape. One appliance manufacturer, foreseeing this problem, produces sandwich plates with three different patterns. But if your appliance lacks this variety, disguise the shape of your culinary creations under concealing, though relevant garnishes.

Brush the tops of sweet pies with honey and sprinkle them with nuts, pipe sweet spicy orange butter over apple pies — it will melt marvellously as they go to the table — or pipe herb or spiced butter — paprika butter sharpened with a little soured cream, maybe — over pork or fish pasties. And as a last resort, of course, there is always the all-enveloping lettuce leaf, well-placed slice of tomato, and a host of other ideas in Chapter Six.

3   Grilling Meat and Fish

Honey-glazed lamb cutlets with mint mayonnaise; fillet steak with orange butter; parcels of chicken and golden exotic fruits; plates of tempting, sizzling party snacks; trout with fennel sauce, and colourful, zingy, fish kebabs — it's a deliciously healthy way to cook meat and fish.

No-one who's the proud owner of a contact grill needs to be told how to plain-grill these main high-protein ingredients. The instruction booklet that comes with the appliance will have a complete timetable of cooking temperatures and times. Do follow the one that relates to your own equipment — though never with such blind faith that the first time you grill a chop or a whole fish you don't bother to check at intervals to see if it's ready. I found that the times given in one booklet would have left me, if I hadn't gone prodding about with a skewer, with partly-cooked chicken joints and nearly raw herrings. It is best to make a note of the times that give the results you enjoy, for the exact time varies according to several factors — the age and quality of the meat, the thickness of the cut and, in the case of lamb and beef, the degree of 'rareness' you find acceptable. With fish, age and thickness are the important time-telling factors. Overall weight is less significant.

All the recipes in this chapter are cooked between the two grill plates. In those in which the top plate is resting on the food, the phrase 'in close contact' is used. Appliance manufacturers have their own ways of describing the various positions of the grill — this one seems so self-explanatory, it surely cannot cause confusion.

Throughout the chapter there are ideas for marinades, the sauce that imparts flavour before cooking, and can then be used for basting during cooking, or as a serving sauce. These marinades fulfil several purposes. The oil content helps to moisturize 'dry' foods, like poultry and white fish; the acid, be it wine, fruit juice or vinegar, helps to offset richness — the fat or oil in pork, mackerel and herring, for example; and the flavourings — herbs, spices, honey, sugar — complement the natural flavour of the food: even lend a hand and add flavour where it's lacking. Added to that, all these marinades act as tenderizers — far better to give your steak a sip of wine than to hit it over the head with a hammer!

If you just haven't time to allow the food to steep for several hours before cooking, soak it in the marinade just while you make the salad or set the table — every little helps.

From flavoured sauces to flavoured butters. Here's a way to add personality and style to the plainest of foods. Make a selection of herb, spice and fruit butters and ring the changes, using them as a cooking medium or last-minute garnish, and your food and your reputation as a cook will be transformed.

BARRACK CHOPS

    4 chump chops of lamb
    50g (2 oz) butter
    5 ml (1 teaspoon) curry paste
    1 small onion, grated or finely chopped
    5 ml (1 teaspoon) Worcestershire sauce
    5 ml (1 teaspoon) made mustard
    a pinch of cayenne
    salt and freshly ground black pepper
    mint sprigs, to garnish

For the sauce
>150 ml (¼ pint) plain yoghurt, chilled
>½ small cucumber, peeled and finely diced
>45 ml (3 tablespoons) chopped mint

Heat the contact grill to High.

Beat the butter to soften it, then beat in the remaining ingredients. Spread the chops on both sides with this paste.

Brush both grill plates with oil or butter. Grill the chops, in close contact, for 6 — 8 minutes. Do not allow the chops to overcook, or they toughen.

To make the sauce, mix together the yoghurt, cucumber and mint and season with pepper. Serve well chilled.

Serve the chops garnished with sprigs of mint and the sauce separately.

HONEY CUTLETS

Glazed lamb with an unusual mint sauce.
>8 lamb cutlets, trimmed of excess fat
>50 g (2 oz) butter, softened
>30 ml (2 tablespoons) honey
>15 ml (1 tablespoon) Meaux mustard
>mint sprigs, to garnish

For the sauce
>5 ml (1 teaspoon) clear honey
>15 ml (1 tablespoon) chopped mint
>75 ml (5 tablespoons) mayonnaise

Heat the contact grill to High.

Mix together the butter, honey and mustard and spread the paste on both sides of the cutlets. Brush both grill plates with oil or butter and grill the cutlets, in close contact, for 6 —

8 minutes, depending on the thickness of the meat.

To make the sauce, stir the honey and mint into the mayonnaise.

A decorative way to serve the cutlets is to arrange them in a wheel pattern on a large plate with the mint sprigs between them and the sauce in a small bowl in the centre.

A green salad with orange segments goes well with this dish.

GREEN PEPPER LAMB

This is more 'special' than chops, and quite different enough for a dinner party.

900 g (2 lb) cut from lean leg of lamb (2 slices about 2.5 cm
  (1 in) thick)
60 ml (4 tablespoons) olive oil
50 g (2 oz) green peppercorns, very lightly crushed
2.5 ml (½ teaspoon) dried rosemary, crumbled
45 ml (3 tablespoons) mayonnaise
15 ml (1 tablespoon) green herb mustard

Heat the contact grill to High.

Cut the meat into four 'steaks'. Brush each one with the olive oil on both sides. On a plate or piece of greaseproof paper, mix together the peppercorns and rosemary. Press the lamb into this mixture so that it is 'pitted' with the flavouring on both sides; pat the peppercorns well into the meat.

Arrange the lamb on the lower grill plate and grill it between the plates, in close contact, for 3 minutes. Half-turn the pieces of lamb so that the 'stripes' from the grill plates come at right angles. Continue cooking for about 3 minutes more, or until the lamb is just as you like it.

Stir the mayonnaise and mustard together and place a spoonful on each lamb steak just as you serve it.

FILLET STEAK WITH ORANGE BUTTER

Grilled steak *can* be dry — but not if it has been marinated in oil and wine.

    4 fillet steaks, about 175 g (6 oz) each
    50 g (2oz) orange garlic butter (page 51), to serve
    watercress sprigs, to garnish

For the marinade
    30 ml (2 tablespoons) vegetable oil
    75 ml (5 tablespoons) red wine
    grated rind and juice of ½ orange
    1 garlic clove, crushed
    1.5 ml (¼ teaspoon) curry powder (mild or hot, to taste)
    salt and freshly ground black pepper
    1 small onion, grated or finely chopped
    1 bay leaf, crumbled

Tie round the fillet steaks with fine twine to neaten and hold their shape. Mix all the marinade ingredients together in a shallow dish. Arrange the steaks in the marinade, cover with foil and leave at room temperature for at least 4 hours. Turn the steaks as often as you can.

Heat the contact grill to High.

Take the steaks from the marinade and pat them dry with kitchen paper. Brush the grill plates with oil. Grill the steaks, in close contact, for 3 minutes. Baste them with the marinade and half-turn them on the grill plate, to get the criss-cross effect. Grill for a further 2 — 4 minutes, according to the thickness of the meat and how 'rare' or well-done you like it to be. Remove the strings.

Serve each steak topped with a pat of orange garlic butter and garnished with watercress sprigs.

TRELLIS STEAK

4 slices sirloin steak, about 175 g (6 oz) each
freshly ground black pepper
5 ml (1 teaspoon) dried thyme flowers
40 g (½ oz) parsley butter (page 50)
8 anchovy fillets
10 stuffed olives, halved
10 ml (2 teaspoons) chopped parsley, to garnish

Heat the contact grill to High.

Brush the grill plates with oil or butter. Well season the steaks on both sides with pepper (but not with salt) and sprinkle on the thyme flowers.

Spread parsley butter on the steaks and grill them between the plates, in close contact, for 3 minutes. Give the steaks a half-turn to get the criss-cross lines. Top them with more parsley butter and grill for a further 2 − 5 minutes, depending on the thickness of the meat and your preference.

Cut the anchovy fillets in halves lengthways. Arrange four strips on each steak, in a noughts and crosses pattern, with olive halves in alternate spaces. Sprinkle with the chopped parsley and serve very hot.

IMPROVED STEAK

700 g (1½ lb) rump steak, cut into 4 slices
4 spring onions, finely chopped
3 garlic cloves, crushed
60 ml (4 tablespoons) vegetable oil
30 ml (2 tablespoons) beef stock, or red wine
freshly ground black pepper
40 g (1½ oz) watercress butter (page 51), to serve
watercress sprigs, to garnish

Heat the contact grill to High.

Lightly score the meat in slashes on both sides. Mix the remaining ingredients (except the watercress butter and watercress sprigs) together in a shallow dish and turn the meat in this basting sauce to moisten it thoroughly on both sides.

Brush both grill plates with oil or butter. Grill the steak, in close contact, for 3 minutes, give it a half-turn and brush it again with the sauce. Grill for a further 2 − 5 minutes according to the thickness of the meat and the degree of 'rareness' or 'doneness' you enjoy.

Serve the steak with a pat of watercress butter on each portion − add it only just on the point of serving − and garnish with watercress sprigs.

SPICED BEEF SKEWERS

    12 small onions, skinned
    450 g (1 lb) minced beef
    50 g (2 oz) breadcrumbs
    15 ml (1 tablespoon) chopped parsley
    15 ml (1 tablespoon) Worcestershire sauce
    salt and freshly ground black pepper
    flour, to coat
    4 bay leaves

For the sauce
    30 ml (2 tablespoons) Worcestershire sauce
    30 ml (2 tablespoons) tomato purée
    2.5 ml (½ teaspoon) French mustard
    15 ml (1 tablespoon) soft dark brown sugar
    10 ml (2 teaspoons) lemon juice
    60 ml (4 tablespoons) chicken stock, or water

Boil the onions in water for about 3 minutes, to partly cook them and mellow the flavour. Mix together the minced beef, breadcrumbs, parsley and Worcestershire sauce and season with salt and pepper. Beat the mixture together very well until it forms a sticky paste. Shape it into 16 small balls and roll them in flour to coat them thoroughly. Thread four skewers with the meat balls, onions and a bay leaf.

Heat the contact grill to High.

Put all the sauce ingredients into a small pan, stir to dissolve the sugar and bring just to the boil. Baste the skewers with this sauce.

Brush the lower grill plate with oil, arrange the skewers and cook them, between the grill plates, for about 8 minutes. During this time baste the skewers with the sauce and turn them over once.

As always with kebabs, rice is a good accompaniment. So is plain yoghurt stirred with finely-diced cucumber and chopped mint (page 28).

HAWAIIAN CHICKEN PARCELS

A dish that is all sweetness and light — the sweetness of mixed exotic fruits and the light, accompanying sauce.

4 chicken joints, skinned
30 ml (2 tablespoons) vegetable oil
15 ml (1 tablespoon) soy sauce
15 ml (1 tablespoon) clear honey
2 bananas, halved
4 peaches, skinned, stoned and halved
1 orange, skinned and segmented
mixed spice
mint sprigs, to garnish

Heat the contact grill to High.

Cut four pieces of foil about 30 cm (12 in) square. Prick the chicken joints all over — viciously! — with a sterilized darning needle. This helps the flavour. Mix together the oil, soy sauce and honey. Put one chicken joint in the centre of each foil square and brush the meat on all sides with the sauce mixture. Divide the fruit between the 4 portions and sprinkle it very lightly with spice. Close up the foil and seal the joins to make them moisture-proof. Arrange the parcels on the grill.

Cook the chicken, in close contact with the grill plates, for 20 − 25 minutes, until the meat is thoroughly cooked. Open one parcel and test with a skewer or sharp knife.

Slit open the parcels and top each one with a sprig of mint. Cooked this way, the chicken is delicious with buttery noodles.

CHICKEN KEBABS WITH PEANUT SAUCE

Derived from Satay Ajam, an Indonesian dish.

3 chicken breasts
45 ml (3 tablespoons) soy sauce
45 ml (3 tablespoons) water
2 garlic cloves, crushed
15 ml (1 tablespoon) chopped coriander leaves, or
    crushed coriander seeds

For the sauce
100 g (4 oz) desiccated coconut
150 ml (¼ pint) boiling water
150 g (5 oz) unsalted peanuts
30 ml (2 tablespoons) vegetable oil
1 small onion, chopped
2.5 ml (½ teaspoon) chilli powder
10 ml (2 teaspoons) soft dark brown sugar
15 ml (1 tablespoon) lemon juice
15 ml (1 tablespoon) soy sauce

Skin the chicken, cut the meat from the bones and cut it into 2.5 cm (1 in) cubes. Thread the meat on to four small skewers. Mix the soy sauce, water, garlic and coriander together, pour it into a shallow dish and arrange the skewers in a single layer. Turn them in the marinade. Leave the chicken to take up the flavour while you make the sauce.

Put the coconut in a bowl, pour on the boiling water and leave to infuse for 30 minutes. In a blender, make a paste with the peanuts, oil, onion, chilli and sugar. Scrape the paste into a small pan. Strain the liquid from the coconut into the pan, pressing it well against the sieve to extract maximum moisture and flavour. Stir well and bring the sauce just to the boil. Set it aside to keep warm.

Heat the contact grill to High.

Brush the lower grill plate with oil. Arrange the skewers on the plate, brush them with any remaining marinade and cook them, between the grill plates, for about 5 — 7 minutes, or until the chicken is cooked.

Stir the lemon juice and soy sauce into the peanut sauce and serve it separately.

This very tasty combination of kebabs and sauce is good with plenty of rice, and contrasting side dishes of raw onion rings, sliced hard-boiled egg, sliced banana tossed in desiccated coconut, and thinly sliced tomatoes.

CHICKEN BREASTS WITH ORANGE

50 g (2 oz) butter
4 chicken breasts, skinned
10 ml (2 teaspoons) chopped parsley
10 ml (2 teaspoons) chopped marjoram
10 ml (2 teaspoons) lemon balm
4 small bay leaves
30 ml (2 tablespoons) orange juice
salt and freshly ground black pepper
2 oranges, peeled and thinly sliced
5 ml (1 teaspoon) flour and a small knob of butter, optional

Heat the contact grill to High.

Cut four pieces of foil about 25 cm (10 in) square and grease them well. Arrange one chicken piece in the centre of each piece of foil. Divide the herbs, butter and orange juice between them. Season the chicken with salt and pepper and cover each one with slices of orange. Fold the foil over and make tightly-sealed parcels.

Arrange the parcels in the baking dish and cook them between the plates for 20 — 25 minutes, or until the chicken is thoroughly cooked. (Test it by piercing with a skewer or sharp knife. The juices should be colourless, and not red.)

Either serve the parcels still sealed with the aroma and surprise intact, or, if you prefer a thicker sauce, transfer the chicken pieces and orange slices to a heated serving dish. Strain the juices into a small pan. Mix together the flour and butter, add to the sauce and stir until it thickens. Pour over the chicken.

You can cook tomatoes, mushrooms or courgettes in the baking dish at the same time. Brush the vegetables with butter and sprinkle them with herbs.

CHICKEN AND HAM BURGERS

Make them yourself and they can be really rather special.

    2 large chicken joints
    450 g (1 lb) unsmoked gammon
    freshly ground black pepper
    15 ml (1 tablespoon) chopped parsley
    5 ml (1 teaspoon) grated orange rind
    vegetable oil, for brushing
    50 g (2 oz) butter
    2 large onions, thinly sliced into rings
    2 large cooking apples, peeled, cored and sliced into rings

Skin the chicken and cut the meat from the bones. Trim the fat from the gammon. Mince the meats together and put them into a bowl. Using a wooden spoon, pound them together until they are well blended and form a thick paste. Season the mixture with pepper, the parsley and the orange rind. Divide the mixture into eight and shape into flat burgers.

Heat the contact grill to High.

Brush both grill plates with oil and grill the burgers, in close contact, for about 5 minutes, or until they are crisp on the outside. Remove the burgers and keep them warm.

Melt the butter in a small pan and toss the onion and apple rings to coat them thoroughly. Arrange them on the grill plate, dust them with pepper and grill then between the plates for about 3 minutes, untill they are toffee brown.

Serve the burgers hot, piled with onion and apple rings. Spicy mango or peach chutney is a good accompaniment.
Makes 8 burgers

GRILLED TURKEY 'ESCALLOPES' WITH CHERRY MAYONNAISE

Cold sauces can be delicious with 'dry' meat dishes; just your luck, they're quicker, too.

  4 portions of turkey breast
  salt and freshly ground black pepper
  a pinch of ground coriander
  40 g (2 oz) butter, melted
  watercress sprigs, to garnish

For the sauce
  150 ml (¼ pint) mayonnaise
  225 g (8 oz) canned pitted Morello cherries, very well
    drained

Heat the contact grill to High.

Season the turkey breasts well with salt, pepper and a pinch of coriander and brush them on both sides with the melted butter.

Brush the grill plates with oil or butter. Grill the turkey, in close contact with both plates, for 2 minutes. Give the turkey pieces a half-turn, to get the brown criss-cross effect. Grill them for a further 2 — 3 minutes, until they are brown outside but still slightly moist — though not pink — inside.

To make the sauce, dry the cherries on kitchen paper and stir them into the mayonnaise. Put just a small blob of sauce on each turkey portion, with the watercress to garnish, and serve the rest separately.

New potatoes and green salad complete a delicious 'in-a-trice' meal.

PORK CHOPS WITH MUSTARD JACKETS

    4 large pork chops
    40 g (1½ oz) butter
    30 ml (2 tablespoons) Dijon mustard
    5 ml (1 teaspoon) mustard powder
    salt and freshly ground black pepper
    8 large mushrooms, sliced
    25 g (1 oz) mustard butter (page 51)
    30 ml (2 tablespoons) double cream, whipped
    watercress sprigs, to garnish
    1 lemon, quartered, to garnish

Heat the contact grill to High.

Cut four pieces of foil about 25 cm (10 in) square and grease them.

Snip the rim of pork fat at intervals to prevent it from curling. Beat the butter to soften it and stir in the mustards and the salt and pepper. Spread the paste on to both sides of each chop.

Grill the chops between the grill plates, in close contact, for 5 minutes. Lower the heat to Medium. Transfer the chops to the foil squares, divide the mushrooms between them, and top each one with a pat of the mustard butter. Seal up the foil to make neat, tight parcels, return them to the grill and cook for a further 8 — 10 minutes, or until the meat is thoroughly cooked.

Before serving, slit open the parcels, top each chop with a blob of cream and garnish with watercress. Serve with a wedge of lemon.

This is the way to achieve the best of both worlds. The chops are first browned and sealed and then, more gently, cooked in buttery juices.

As an alternative
Cook veal chops in the same way.

PORK AND DRIED FRUIT KEBABS

700 g (1½ lb) pork fillet
8 prunes, stoned (some need pre-soaking)
12 whole dried apricots, soaked and drained
1 green pepper, de-seeded and cut into squares

For the marinade
45 ml (3 tablespoons) vegetable oil
grated rind and juice of 1 orange
15 ml (1 tablespoon) red wine vinegar
salt and freshly ground black pepper

Trim fat from the pork and cut the meat into 2.5 cm (1 in) cubes.

Mix together the oil, orange rind and juice, vinegar, salt and pepper. Put it into a polythene bag, add the pork cubes and tie the top securely. Leave the pork to marinate for about 4 hours. Open the bag to add the stoned prunes and whole apricots, re-tie it, shake it well and leave for about another 2 hours. Strain the pork and fruit and reserve the marinade.

Heat the contact grill to Medium.

Thread the pork, prunes, apricots and green pepper on to four skewers. Brush the lower grill plate with oil or butter. Grill the kebabs, between the grill plates, for 7 — 9 minutes, turning them often and basting them with any remaining marinade.

Serve the kebabs on a bed of rice.

DEVILLED GAMMON STEAKS

Two 225 g (8 oz) gammon steaks
25 g (1 oz) butter, melted
30 ml (2 tablespoons) English mustard
50 g (2 oz) demerara sugar
4 canned pineapple rings, drained

Heat the contact grill to High.

Snip the fat all round the gammon to prevent it from curling. Mix together the butter, mustard and 40 g (1½ oz) of the sugar and spread the paste generously over both sides of the gammon. Brush both grill plates with oil or butter.

Arrange the steaks on the lower grill plate with the pineapple rings around them. Sprinkle the fruit with the remaining sugar. Grill between the two plates, in close contact, for 6 — 8 minutes, until the gammon is cooked. Half-turn each piece once, for the criss-cross-lined effect.

Cut each piece in half and garnish each portion with a pineapple ring.

BACON AND BANANA ROLLS

4 long, thin 'sausage-shaped' bread rolls
8 rashers streaky bacon
20 ml (4 teaspoons) soft dark brown sugar

   10 ml (2 teaspoons) mustard powder
   5 ml (1 teaspoon) malt vinegar
   4 small bananas
   50 g (2 oz) mustard butter (page 51)

Heat the contact grill to High.

Wrap the bread rolls in foil, put them in the baking dish and heat them between the grill plates.

Cut the rind from the bacon. Using a blunt knife, flatten and stretch the bacon rashers. Mix the sugar, mustard and vinegar to a paste and spread it over the bacon. Skin the bananas and wrap two rashers of bacon, mustard sides out, around each banana. Secure them with wooden cocktail sticks if necessary.

Remove the bread rolls from the heat. Place the banana rolls in the baking dish and cook, between the plates, for about 4 − 6 minutes, or until the bacon is crispy.

Split the bread rolls and spread them with the mustard butter. Remove the cocktail sticks. Push a banana roll into each and serve very hot, with mustard.

'Finger' salads, like sticks of celery, slices of cucumber and matchsticks of raw carrot, are just right with this very tasty snack.

PARTY PIECES

When you're giving a drinks party or an informal brunch, lunch or supper, it's fun to have a selection of grilled savouries. Made in moments and served piping hot, they have everything going for them. You can use either your contact grill or sandwich maker for them.

Angels on horseback
   10 rashers streaky bacon
   20 canned smoked oysters, drained

Apple rings
> 10 rashers streaky bacon
> 20 thick slices dessert apple, cored

Artichoke rolls
> 10 rashers streaky bacon
> 10 canned artichoke hearts, drained and halved

Bacon fondue
> 10 rashers streaky bacon
> 20 2.5–4 cm (1–1½ in) cubes cheese (Gruyère or Edam)

Bacon croûtons
> 10 rashers streaky bacon
> 15 ml (1 tablespoon) chopped parsley
> 2 garlic cloves, crushed
> 20 2.5 cm (1 in) cubes bread

Mix together the parsley and garlic and toss the bread cubes in it to coat them.

Devils on horseback
> 10 rashers streaky bacon
> 20 prunes, stoned (some need pre-soaking)
> 20 blanched almonds

Liver and bacon rolls
> 10 rashers streaky bacon
> 225g (8 oz) lamb's liver

Sausage and bacon rolls
> 10 rashers streaky bacon
> 20 cocktail sausages

Pineapple rings
> 10 rashers streaky bacon
> 20 chunks of pineapple, drained

Heat the contact grill to High.

Cut the rinds from the bacon, stretch the rashers (see previous recipe) and cut each one in two. Roll the bacon round the appropriate filling – a piece of bread, liver, an oyster, and so on. Thread the rolls on skewers or cocktail sticks. You can prepare them in advance to this stage, and leave them wrapped in foil in the refrigerator.

Arrange the sticks on the lower grill plate and grill them, between the two plates, for 3 – 4 minutes, turning them once, until the bacon is crispy.

Serve the rolls hot, on cocktail sticks, or on toast rounds. Stamp out mini rounds of bread, using a small biscuit cutter, and toast them.

Each 'recipe' makes 20 small rolls

FRESH HADDOCK WITH ANCHOVIES

700 g (1½lb) fresh haddock, skinned

For the marinade
30 ml (2 tablespoons) vegetable oil
15 ml (1 tablespoon) cider vinegar
90 ml (6 tablespoons) dry cider
10 ml (2 teaspoons) fresh rosemary
salt and freshly ground black pepper

50 g (2 oz) anchovy butter (page 49), to serve
1 lemon, quartered, to garnish

Cut the haddock into slices about 10 cm (4 in) wide and arrange them in a shallow dish. Mix all the marinade ingredients together, pour over the fish and cover. Leave in the refrigerator for at least 2 hours, basting the fish with the marinade if it's convenient.

Heat the contact grill to Medium.

Strain the fish from the marinade and pat it dry with

kitchen paper. Brush the grill plates with butter. Grill the fish with the top plate lowered but not in close contact, for 3 minutes. Baste the fish with marinade and cook for a further 3–4 minutes, until the fish is just firm to the touch.

Serve the fish topped with pats of anchovy butter and with lemon wedges.

As an alternative
You could, of course, use any other white fish, such as cod fillet or cod steaks.

FISH KEBABS

> 450 g (1 lb) cod fillet, or other white fish
> 60 ml (4 tablespoons) vegetable oil
> grated rind and juice of 1 lemon
> 1 bay leaf, crumbled
> 5 ml (1 teaspoon) fennel seed, crushed
> salt and freshly ground black pepper
> 4 courgettes, cut into 2.5 cm (1 in) slices
> 8 small tomatoes
> 1 lemon, quartered

Heat the contact grill to High.

Cut the fish into 4 cm (1½ in) chunks. Mix together the oil, lemon rind and juice, bay leaf and fennel seed and season with salt and pepper.

Divide the pieces of fish, the courgettes and the tomatoes between 4 skewers and brush them liberally with the fennel sauce. Brush the lower grill plate with oil or butter.

Arrange the skewers on the grill, lower the top plate and grill the kebabs for 3 minutes. Brush them with the sauce, turn the skewers and grill for a further 2 – 3 minutes, or until the fish is just tender. Impale one piece of lemon on each skewer.

These kebabs look good arranged on a bed of shredded lettuce.

SALMON FLORENTINE

Salmon is so quick and easy to grill. Here's a nutritious and colourful way to present it.

    4 salmon steaks, about 2.5 cm (1 in) thick
    900 g (2 lb) spinach, washed and drained
    75 g (3 oz) tarragon or mint butter (page 50)
    salt and freshly ground black pepper
    60 ml (4 tablespoons) double cream

Heat the contact grill to Medium.

Season the salmon steaks. Brush both grill plates with oil or butter. Arrange the salmon on the lower plate and dot each portion with about 15 g (½ oz) herb butter. Grill between the plates, in close contact, for 8 — 10 minutes.

Meanwhile, put the spinach in a pan over a fairly high heat. After 2 minutes, reduce the heat. Stir it well and cook for a further 8 — 10 minutes, until it is 'collapsed' and tender.

Turn the cooked spinach into a colander and drain it thoroughly. Return to the pan, add the cream, season with salt and pepper and mix well. Stir for a few seconds over low heat. Transfer the spinach to a warmed serving dish. Arrange the cooked salmon steaks on the vegetable and put a pat of the remaining herb butter on each portion just before serving.

GRILLED TROUT WITH FENNEL SAUCE

    4 medium-sized trout
    4 sprigs fennel, or other fresh herb
    salt and freshly ground black pepper
    50 g (2oz) fennel or other herb butter (page 50)
    1 lemon, quartered, to serve

For the sauce

    150 ml (¼ pint) soured cream

    5 ml (1 teaspoon) very finely chopped fennel, or other
        matching herb (as above)

    5 ml (1 teaspoon) lemon juice

Heat the contact grill to Medium.

Gut and clean the trout, place a sprig of herb in each cavity, season the fish with salt and pepper and dot the herb butter over them.

Brush the grill plates with oil or butter and grill the trout, in close contact, for about 5 – 6 minutes, according to size.

To make the sauce, stir together the soured cream, herb and lemon juice and season with salt and pepper.

Serve the sauce separately. Garnish the fish with the lemon wedges.

TROUT IN A BLANKET

    4 medium-sized trout, gutted and cleaned

    25 g (1 oz) parsley butter (page 50), softened

    4 sprigs of fennel or rosemary

    8 – 12 rashers streaky bacon, de-rinded

    1 lemon, quartered, to garnish

Heat the contact grill to Medium.

Spread the softened butter in the cavities of the trout and put a sprig of herb inside each one. Stretch the bacon rashers, using a blunt knife, and wrap them round the trout to cover the fish completely.

Brush both grill plates with oil or butter. Arrange the trout on the lower plate and grill, in close contact, for about 7 – 9 minutes, according to size.

Serve the fish garnished with the lemon wedges. Horse-radish or apple sauce are both good accompaniments.

As an alternative
Other fish is good cooked this way, too. Bacon has quite an affinity. Try wrapping thick slices of fresh or smoked haddock, cod or coley. The fat from the bacon both moistens and flavours the fish — it's a good combination.

OLD-FASHIONED HERRINGS

Often the old ways are the best!

> 4 medium-sized herrings
> 25 g (1 oz) butter
> 50 g (2 oz) mushrooms, chopped
> 25 g (1 oz) rolled porridge oats
> 5 ml (1 teaspoon) chopped parsley
> grated rind and juice of ½ lemon
> salt and freshly ground black pepper

Heat the contact grill to Medium.

Cut four pieces of foil about 23 × 30 cm (12 × 9 in) and grease them well.

Cut off the fish heads, gut and clean the fish. Split them open and remove the backbone. Or ask the fishmonger to do this for you.

Melt the butter in a small pan on a grill plate and stir in all the remaining ingredients except the lemon juice. Place one fish on each piece of foil. Divide the oat filling between them, packing it into the cavity. Close the fish again and sprinkle them with the lemon juice. Close up the foil parcels and make double joins to secure them.

Arrange the parcels on the lower grill plate and cook them between the plates in close contact for about 12 — 14 minutes, or until the fish are well cooked. Check one parcel to test.

Lots of hot, crusty rolls and a bowl of salad are my favourite accompaniments.

MACKEREL AND GRAPEFRUIT KEBABS

The richness of the fish is amply compensated for by the tangy fruit.

350 g (12 oz) mackerel fillets
8 small firm tomatoes
100 g (4 oz) button mushrooms, halved if large
1 green pepper, de-seeded and cut into 4 cm (1½ in) squares
2 grapefruit, peeled and segmented

For the marinade
30 ml (2 tablespoons) olive oil
30 ml (2 tablespoons) orange juice
15 ml (1 tablespoon) medium sherry
5 ml (1 teaspoon) soft dark brown sugar
15 ml (1 tablespoon) chopped parsley, or 5 ml (1 teaspoon) dried parsley
15 ml (1 tablespoon) chopped thyme, or 5 ml (1 teaspoon) dried thyme
a pinch of cayenne

Mix all the marinade ingredients together in a shallow dish.

Skin the fish fillets and cut them into 4 cm (1½ in) pieces. Thread the fish, tomatoes, mushrooms, pepper and grapefruit on to four skewers. Arrange the skewers in the marinade and brush it over them. Cover and set aside for about 2 hours, turning the kebabs once or twice if possible.

Heat the contact grill to High.

Place the kebabs on the grill plate and baste them with the remaining marinade. Grill between the two plates for about 5–6 minutes, until the mackerel is cooked and the grapefruit is crispy brown. Baste the kebabs with the remaining marinade and turn them once during this time. Serve very hot.

These are good with rice and green salad.

FLAVOURED BUTTERS AND SAUCES

Even the simplest grilled food is doubly delicious when it is cooked or served with a flavoured butter or sauce. It adds moisture to dry meats and fish – poultry, cod, haddock and others – and positiviely makes *everything* glisten. You can make the butters in 100 g (4 oz) or 225 g (8 oz) quantities, wrap them in foil and store them in the refrigerator or freezer.

Recipes in this chapter give ideas for using herb, spice or fruit-flavoured butters to brush on food when cooking, to wrap into foil parcels, or to garnish, when it melts its way tantalizingly over every inviting surface.

Always use unsalted butter, and have it at room temperature. Beat it with a wooden spoon, in an electric mixer or in a food processor until it is softened. If there is some lemon or orange juice in the recipe, add it slowly, drop by drop, or the butter will separate. Beat in the other ingredients. Then shape the butter into a roll, wrap in film or foil and chill in the refrigerator, or freeze. Or, to pipe it into rosettes or other decorative shapes, spoon it into a piping bag without chilling.

Anchovy butter
    100 g (4 oz) unsalted butter, softened
    6 anchovy fillets, pounded
    5 ml (1 teaspoon) lemon juice
    10 ml (2 teaspoons) chopped parsley

To serve with grilled white fish, steaks or veal.

Cucumber herb butter
    100 g (4 oz) unsalted butter, softened
    10 ml (2 teaspoons) chopped fennel or dill
    ½ a small cucumber, peeled, seeded and finely diced
    grated rind and juice of ½ lemon
    salt and freshly ground black pepper

To serve with white fish, salmon and spicy meats.

Devilled butter
>   100 g (4 oz) unsalted butter, softened
>   30 ml (2 tablespoons) Worcestershire sauce
>   10 ml (2 teaspoons) mustard powder
>   a few drops of lemon juice

To serve with meat and white fish.

Garlic butter
>   100 g (4 oz) unsalted butter, softened
>   4 garlic cloves, crushed
>   grated rind and juice of ½ lemon
>   salt and freshly ground black pepper

To serve with all meats, but especially steak.

Herb butter
>   100 g (4 oz) unsalted butter, softened
>   30 ml (2 tablespoons) chopped herbs — basil, fennel, marjoram, mint, parsley, tarragon, thyme, or a mixture of herbs
>   5 ml (1 teaspoon) lemon juice
>   1 garlic clove, crushed (optional)
>   salt and freshly ground black pepper

To serve with all meats and fish.

Honey butter
>   100 g (4 oz) unsalted butter, softened
>   30 ml (2 tablespoons) honey
>   5 ml (1 teaspoon) lemon juice
>   a pinch of mixed spice

To serve with grilled white fish or poultry.

Orange cashew butter
>   100 g (4 oz) unsalted butter, softened
>   grated rind of 1 orange

a pinch of grated nutmeg
50 g (2 oz) ground cashew nuts
salt and freshly ground black pepper

To serve with veal or poultry.

Orange garlic butter
100 g (4 oz) unsalted butter, softened
grated rind of 2 oranges
2 garlic cloves, crushed
30 ml (2 tablespoons) chopped parsley, or chives
salt and freshly ground black pepper

To serve with poultry, fish, pork, game.

Spiced butter
100 g (4 oz) unsalted butter, softened
5–10 ml (1–2 teaspoons) ground spice – cinnamon, curry
    powder, mustard powder or made mustards, or
    paprika
5 ml (1 teaspoon) lemon juice
a pinch of grated orange rind

To serve with grilled fruits (cinnamon); steak, chops,
poultry, fish (curry, mustard or paprika).

Watercress butter
100 g (4 oz) unsalted butter, softened
10 ml (2 teaspoons) grated onion
1 bunch watercress sprigs, very finely chopped
salt and freshly ground black pepper

To serve with steak.

Quick herb or spiced butters
Cut well-chilled butter into cubes or pats and roll them in
finely chopped herbs or ground spice.

Barbecue sauce (1)

You can use some of the sauce to brush meats before grilling and serve the remainder separately.

   10 ml (2 teaspoons) English mustard
   15 ml (1 tablespoon) honey
   5 ml (1 teaspoon) Worcestershire sauce
   60 ml (4 tablespoons) tomato juice
   10 ml (2 teaspoons) lemon juice
   1 small onion, grated
   10 ml (2 teaspoons) soft dark brown sugar
   45 ml (3 tablespoons) water

Put all the ingredients into a small pan and bring to the boil.

Barbecue sauce (2)

Specially good with white fish.

   25 g (1 oz) butter
   150 ml (¼ pint) red wine
   5 ml (1 teaspoon) made mustard
   5 ml (1 teaspoon) chilli sauce
   15 ml (1 tablespoon) lemon juice
   10 ml (2 teaspoons) soft dark brown sugar
   2.5 ml (½ teaspoon) salt

Heat all the ingredients in a small pan, bring to the boil and simmer for 10 minutes.

Sweet spicy sauce

Here's a good one to serve with lamb, veal and poultry.

   45 ml (3 tablespoons) mango or peach chutney, finely
      chopped
   30 ml (2 tablespoons) Worcestershire sauce
   15 ml (1 tablespoon) soy sauce
   15 ml (1 tablespoon) tomato purée

30 ml (2 tablespoons) red wine
1.5 ml (¼ teaspoon) cayenne
5 ml (1 teaspoon) soft dark brown sugar
1 small onion, grated
25 g (1 oz) butter
1.5 ml (¼ teaspoon) salt

Put all the ingredients into a small pan, bring to the boil and simmer very gently for 5 minutes, stirring occasionally. The sauce should be thick and syrupy.

Spiced yoghurt marinade
150 ml (¼ pint) plain yoghurt
15 ml (1 tablespoon) curry powder (mild or hot, to taste)
1.5 ml (¼ teaspoon) ground cinnamon
1.5 ml (¼ teaspoon) ground ginger
1.5 ml (¼ teaspoon) ground black pepper
15 ml (1 tablespoon) vegetable oil
15 ml (1 tablespoon) lemon juice
15 ml (1 tablespoon) tomato purée

Mix all the ingredients together. Use as a basting paste for kebabs or grilled meats, or heat in a small pan and serve as an accompanying sauce.

4　'Oven' Meals

Veal moussaka with a cheesy yoghurt topping; a piece of brisket cooked to perfection with all its natural 'juices'; pieces of chicken coated with crunchy sesame seeds; pheasant with honeyed grapes; and fillets of fish rolled round a fragrant filling — there's no end to the versatility of the contact grill.

All the recipes in this chapter are for meat or fish, whether it's poultry, game, red meat or offal, whole oily fish or delicate fish fillets. And they are all cooked in a baking dish on the contact grill, between the top and bottom grill plates. Used this way, the appliance truly thinks it's an oven. With heat coming from both sides, and the source of heat very close to the food, there's no wastage of fuel or time.

Get used to stir-frying the vegetables in the baking dish, sealing the exposed surface of meat or fish to trap in all the flavours, and then stirring in the liquid to make the sauce; cooking for a while, a very little while, and then maybe adding a crunchy topping — this way the appliance takes the place of hotplate, oven and grill to cook a single dish.

To fry-start the dishes in the baking dish on the lower grill plate, you can have the top plate in the open position — this is probably easier when the ingredients need frequent stirring or are added at frequent intervals. Otherwise — as when pre-cooking the aubergines for moussaka — close down the top plate and you almost double the heat factor.

Always check the size of the main ingredient — pieces of

chicken, rabbit portions, or whole fish — against the size of your baking dish before launching into a recipe. If it's a tight fit, especially as far as height is concerned, it might be necessary to snip off a wayward bone, cut the joints into smaller portions, cut off the fish heads, or whatever. It is far better to get these mechanics out of the way before you start cooking.

With cooking time pared down to the minimum like this, there isn't much time, when you come to think of it, for the meat and fish to absorb the flavours of the herbs, spices, vegetables or cooking liquids. That's why many of the dishes are marinated in a mixture of, say, oil, wine and herbs, for a few hours before. Toss the meat or fish in this flavouring blend the morning or the evening before the meal and half the job's done. In most cases you just have to pop the dish in the grill when you're ready. The marinade becomes the sauce, and raw flavours become mellow.

ST CLEMENT'S VEAL

The chops are marinated and then cooked in the baking dish. Maximum effect for minimum effort.

    4 veal chops
    5 ml (1 teaspoon) flour
    a small knob of butter
    10 ml (2 teaspoons) soft light brown sugar

For the marinade
    grated rind and juice of 1 orange
    granted rind and juice of ½ lemon
    30 ml (2 tablespoons) vegetable oil
    5 ml (1 teaspoon) soy sauce
    salt and freshly ground black pepper

In the baking dish, mix together the orange and lemon rind and juice, the oil and soy sauce and season with salt and pepper. Put the chops in the marinade and cover the dish with foil or put it in a polythene bag.

Leave the chops in the refrigerator to take up the flavour for at least 2 hours, or overnight if it is more convenient.

Heat the contact grill to High.

Cook the chops in the dish for 15–20 minutes between the grill plates, turning them once.

Mix together the butter and flour to form a paste. Stir it into the marinade and keep stirring for about 2 minutes until it has thickened. Add the sugar, taste the sauce and add more salt and pepper if necessary.

VEAL MOUSSAKA

90 ml (6 tablespoons) vegetable oil
1 aubergine, about 200 g (7 oz), thinly sliced
25 g (1 oz) butter
2 garlic cloves, crushed
1 large onion, thinly sliced
450 g (1 lb) minced raw veal
225 g (8 oz) can tomatoes
30 ml (2 tablespoons) tomato purée
5 ml (1 teaspoon) dried oregano
salt and freshly ground black pepper

For the topping
300 ml (½ pint) plain yoghurt
3 egg yolks
25 g (1 oz) Cheddar cheese, grated

Heat the contact grill to High.

Heat half the oil in the baking dish and fry the aubergine slices in 2 batches for about 5 minutes, with the top grill plate closed, until they are golden brown. Add more oil as needed. Remove them temporarily.

Add the butter to the dish and fry the garlic and onion, stirring, for 2 minutes. Stir in the veal and cook for 3 — 4 minutes, stirring once or twice to seal the meat. Add the tomatoes, tomato purée, oregano, salt and pepper, stir well and bring to the boil.

Remove the dish from the heat. Arrange the aubergine slices in overlapping rings over the meat. Beat together the yoghurt and egg yolks and stir in the cheese. Pour the topping over the aubergines and spread it to cover them completely.

Cook between the grill plates for about 20 minutes.

As an alternative
You can use minced beef or lamb in place of the veal, or a mixture of two meats.

This quantity fills a baking dish 18.5 × 30 cm (7½ × 12 in). Reduce the ingredients proportionately for a smaller one.

VEAL AND BACON PIE

You can make any of your favourite old-fashioned meat pies in this way — surely the quickest and easiest method there is.

> 25 g (1 oz) butter
> 6 rashers streaky bacon, de-rinded and cut into squares
> 450 g (1 lb) pie veal, cut into 4 cm (1½ in) cubes
> 1 large onion, sliced
> 100 g (4 oz) mushrooms, sliced
> 15 ml (1 tablespoon) flour
> 300 ml (½ pint) chicken stock
> 45 ml (3 tablespoons) single cream
> 15 ml (1 tablespoon) chopped parsley, or 5 ml (1 teaspoon) dried parsley

salt and freshly ground black pepper
a pinch of cayenne
225 g (8 oz) shortcrust pastry
milk, for brushing

Heat the contact grill to High.

Melt the butter in the baking dish and fry the bacon, between the grill plates, for 3 minutes. Add the veal — another 3 minutes. Then the onion and mushroom, 2 more minutes.

Stir in the flour and gradually pour on the stock, stirring the while. When the sauce boils, stir in the cream and parsley and season with salt and pepper, and a pinch of cayenne. Cover the dish with foil and cook for 10 minutes.

Roll out the pastry to fit the baking dish. Remove the dish from the heat. Place the pastry so that it rests on the meat and brush the top with milk. Roll the trimmings very thinly and cut leaves or other decorations (there won't be the height for anything elaborate), arrange them on the pastry and brush them with milk.

Cook the pie between the grill plates for about 15 minutes, or until the pastry is cooked and golden brown.

This quantity fills a dish 18.5 × 30 cm (7½ × 12 in). Reduce the amounts proportionately for a smaller one.

BEEF OLIVES

A dish with a long history (it has Medieval origins) brought up to date on our magic appliance.

4 thin slices of topside of beef, about 100 g (4 oz) each, beaten flat
25 g (1 oz) flour
salt and freshly ground black pepper
25 g (1 oz) butter

300 ml (½ pint) beef stock
2 large carrots, sliced
2 small turnips, diced

For the filling
   15 g (½ oz) butter
   1 small onion, chopped
   50 g (2 oz) breadcrumbs
   25 g (1 oz) shredded suet
   50 g (2 oz) seedless raisins
   15 ml (1 tablespoon) chopped parsley
   salt and freshly ground black pepper
   1 egg, lightly beaten

For the sauce
   15 ml (1 tablespoon) tomato purée
   30 ml (2 tablespoons) dry sherry

Heat the contact grill to High.

To make the filling, melt the 15 g (½ oz) butter in the baking dish and fry the onion for 1 – 2 minutes. Tip into a bowl and mix with the remaining filling ingredients, bound to a soft, crumbly mixture with the egg.

Divide the filling between the slices of beef and roll them up into sausage shapes. Secure them with cocktail sticks or tie with thin twine. Season the flour with salt and pepper and toss the beef olives in it to coat them thoroughly.

Melt the 25 g (1 oz) butter in the baking dish and fry the rolls for about 3 minutes, turning them so that they brown evenly. Sprinkle in any remaining flour, pour on the stock and bring the sauce to the boil. Add the carrots and turnips.

Cover the dish and cook the beef between the grill plates for 15 minutes. Lower the heat to Medium. Stir the tomato purée and sherry into the sauce, taste it and add more salt and pepper if needed. Cover the dish again and cook for a further 10 minutes, or until the beef is tender.

BEEF CURRY

45 ml (3 tablespoons) vegetable oil
450 g (1 lb) stewing steak, cut into 2.5 cm (1 in) cubes
2 medium-sized onions, sliced
2.5 ml (½ teaspoon) ground turmeric
2.5 ml (½ teaspoon) ground coriander
2.5 ml (½ teaspoon) ground black pepper
1.5 ml (¼ teaspoon) cayenne
1.5 ml (¼ teaspoon) ground cumin
15 ml (1 tablespoon) curry paste
2 garlic cloves, crushed
300 ml (½ pint) hot water
150 ml (¼ pint) plain yoghurt

Heat the contact grill to High.

Heat the oil in the baking dish and fry the meat, between the grill plates, for about 4 minutes to brown it on all sides. Remove the meat temporarily and fry the onions until they are translucent but not brown. Stir in all the spices and keep stirring for 1 minute, then blend in the curry paste, garlic and hot water. Cover the top with foil and cook for 30 – 40 minutes, or until the meat is tender.

Stir in most of the yoghurt and just heat it through. When you have transferred the curry to a serving dish, top it with a cooling spoonful of yoghurt.

As an alternative
If you haven't time to measure or grind the individual spices, use ready-made curry powder, mild or hot, as you like it. You can stir in 50 g (2 oz) sultanas and 25 g (1 oz) desiccated coconut towards the end of the cooking time to add different flavours, textures, and bulk.

BATTERED BEEF

This is toad-in-the-hole with a difference — a delicious difference.

For the batter
    100 g (4 oz) plain flour
    1.5 ml (¼ teaspoon) salt
    1 egg
    300 ml (½ pint) milk
    freshly ground black pepper
    2.5 ml (½ teaspoon) mixed dried herbs

    15 g (½ oz) lard or dripping
    350 g (12 oz) rump steak, cut into 4 cm (1½ in) cubes
    100 g (4 oz) button mushrooms, sliced

To make the batter, sift together the flour and salt. Beat in the egg and, gradually, the milk. Beat until smooth, then stir in the pepper and herbs. (Or put all the ingredients into a blender, and blend.) Cover and leave to stand for about 1 hour.

Heat the contact grill to High.

Melt the fat in the baking dish and fry the meat, stirring to brown it evenly, for 2 —3 minutes. Add the mushrooms and turn them in the fat. Pour on the batter.

Cook between the grill plates for about 20 minutes, until the batter is only just firm at the centre. It might rise enough to come in contact with the top grill plate. In this case, the pudding will have a brown-ridged top. Slide a plastic spatula between the pudding and the grill plate to release it. As the plates have a non-stick coating, it's no problem.

This amount is for a baking dish 18.5 × 30 cm (7½ × 12 in). Halve the quantity if yours is smaller. There just won't be room for it to rise.

AT-THE-DOUBLE BRISKET

You can cook a fairly large piece of meat in the baking tray between the grill plates. The trick is to fold it rather than roll it.

>   1.4 kg (3 lb) brisket of beef
>   salt and freshly ground black pepper
>   10 — 12 cloves
>   15 ml (1 tablespoon) flour

Heat the contact grill to High.

This method uses a roasting bag. If you do not have one, cook the meat in a very little fat in the foil-covered baking dish, turning it once.

Season the meat generously with salt and pepper and scatter the cloves on top. Fold it to fit the baking dish and the distance between the grill plates. Tie it round with thin twine. Shake the flour into the roasting bag, put in the meat and tie the bag. Make two slashes in the top.

Put the bag in the baking dish and cook for 15 minutes. Lower the heat to Medium and cook for about a further 45 minutes, or until the meat is tender. Test it by piercing with a skewer or knife. The juices should run clear.

Tip the juices from the roasting bag into a heated jug and serve them as the sauce.

If there is room in the baking dish, cook small potatoes, their jackets brushed with butter, for the last 20 minutes.

Horseradish sauce is a traditional accompaniment.

Serves 6

SPRING LAMB ONE-POT

>   15 g (½ oz) butter
>   4 chump chops of lamb
>   4 medium-sized potatoes, peeled and thickly sliced

1 large onion, quartered
4 small leeks, cut into 7.5 cm (3 in) pieces
2 cloves garlic, crushed
2 large tomatoes, skinned and quartered
salt and freshly ground black pepper
15 ml (1 tablespoon) chopped lemon balm, or mint
150 ml (¼ pint) sweet cider

Heat the contact grill to High.

Melt the butter in the baking dish. Put in the chops and fry them for 3 minutes on each side. Add the vegetables, season them with salt and pepper and stir in the herb. Pour on the cider.

Cook between the grill plates for 15 minutes. Lower the heat to Medium and continue cooking for 5 minutes.

ARABIAN LAMB

30 ml (2 tablespoons) vegetable oil
700 g (1½ lb) lean lamb, cut into 4 cm (1½ in) cubes
1 large onion, sliced
1 garlic clove, crushed
5 ml (1 teaspoon) ground turmeric
2.5 ml (½ teaspoon) ground cinnamon
salt and freshly ground black pepper
15 ml (1 tablespoon) flour
300 ml (½ pint) chicken stock
5 ml (1 teaspoon) soft dark brown sugar
12 prunes, stoned (some need pre-soaking)
1 lemon, quartered, to garnish

Heat the contact grill to High.

Heat the oil in the baking dish. Fry the lamb cubes, turning them to brown them evenly, for about 3 minutes. Remove the lamb temporarily, add the onion and garlic, stir and fry for 1 minute. Mix in the spices, salt, pepper and flour and stir for 1 minute. Pour on the stock and stir until the sauce thickens.

Return the lamb to the pan, cover with foil and cook between the grill plates for 10 minutes. Lower the heat to Medium, add the sugar and prunes and cook for a further 10 minutes, or until the lamb is tender and still pink inside. Taste the sauce and add more salt, pepper or sugar, if needed. Serve garnished with the lemon wedges.

For a change
Rice is a good accompaniment. For a change, add the grated rind and the juice of one orange to the water in which you cook it and toss a few toasted almonds in just before serving.

LAMB IN EGG AND LEMON SAUCE

The delicious Balkan flavour is added quickly and easily at the last minute.

    4 rashers streaky bacon, de-rinded and cut in squares
    30 ml (2 tablespoons) vegetable oil
    700 g (1½ lb) lean lamb, cut into 4 cm (1½ in) cubes
    1 medium-sized onion, sliced
    1 garlic clove, crushed
    15 ml (1 tablespoon) flour
    150 ml (¼ pint) dry white wine, or dry cider
    150 ml (¼ pint) plus 30 ml (2 tablespoons) chicken stock
    salt and freshly ground black pepper
    1 bay leaf
    2.5 ml (½ teaspoon) dried basil
    2 egg yolks
    15 ml (1 tablespoon) lemon juice
    15 ml (1 tablespoon) chopped parsley, to garnish

Heat the contact grill to High.

Heat the oil in the baking dish, add the bacon and lamb and fry, stirring once or twice, for 3 minutes. Remove the lamb from the dish temporarily, add the onion and garlic and fry for 1 minute. Stir in the flour, gradually pour on the wine or cider and 150 ml (¼ pint) chicken stock. When the sauce thickens, add the salt and pepper, bay leaf and basil.

Back goes the lamb. Cover the dish with foil and cook between the grill plates for 10 minutes. Lower the heat to Medium and cook for 10 minutes more, or until the lamb is tender but still pink inside.

Transfer the meat to a heated serving dish. Discard the bay leaf. Beat together the egg yolks, lemon juice and remaining chicken stock and beat them into the sauce. Do not allow it to boil — unless you want scrambled eggs! Immediately remove from the heat, pour the sauce over the meat and garnish with parsley.

LAMB IN CAPER SAUCE

    25 g (1 oz) butter
    15 ml (1 tablespoon) vegetable oil
    1 large onion, sliced
    700 g (1½ lb) lean lamb, cut into 4 cm (1½ in) cubes
    15 g (½ oz) flour
    300 ml (½ pint) chicken stock
    salt and freshly ground black pepper
    60 ml (4 tablespoons) capers
    grated rind and juice of ½ lemon
    150 ml (¼ pint) plain yoghurt
    15 ml (1 tablespoon) chopped parsley
    1 hard-boiled egg, sliced, to garnish (optional)

Heat the contact grill to High.

Melt the butter and oil in the baking dish and fry the onion for 1 minute. Do not let it brown. Add the lamb and fry, stirring, for 2 — 3 minutes to seal the outside. Stir in the flour and when it has blended, gradually pour on the stock. Bring to the boil, season the sauce with salt and pepper and stir in the capers. Cover the dish with foil and cook between the grill plates for 10 minutes. Lower the heat to Medium and cook for 10 minutes more or until the lamb is tender and still pink inside. Stir in the yoghurt and parsley and allow just to heat through. Taste the sauce and add more salt and pepper if needed. The capers and yoghurt give the sauce quite a pronounced tang.

Garnish with the egg slices, if you like.

BRONZED LAMB

About 1.2 kg (2¾ lb) piece best end of neck of lamb

For the marinade
grated rind and juice of 1 orange
15 ml (1 tablespoon) vinegar
30 ml (2 tablespoons) soy sauce
30 ml (2 tablespoons) dry sherry
30 ml (2 tablespoons) vegetable oil
30 ml (2 tablespoons) water
15 ml (1 tablespoon) black treacle
2.5 ml (½ teaspoon) mixed spice
2 large onions, sliced

Cut the rack of bones from the lamb. Cut between each bone to separate them. Make deep criss-cross cuts through the skin of the lamb, to give a diamond pattern.

Put the meat, bones and all the marinade ingredients into a large plastic bag, tie the top and leave in the refrigerator all day or overnight. Turn the bag over once or twice if it is convenient.

Heat the contact grill to High.

Put the lamp, skin side up, bones and marinade in the baking dish and check that there is clearance between the meat and the top grill plate. If not, flatten the meat a little.

Cover the dish with foil and cook between the plates for 25 minutes. Remove the foil, baste the lamb with the sauce and cook, without the foil, for a further 5 minutes. The skin should be very brown, glazed and crispy and the meat tender and pink inside.

Serve with rice and a green vegetable or salad. It is quite permissible to gnaw the bones!
Serves 6

PORK STROGONOFF

700 g (1½ lb) fillets (tenderloin) of pork, thinly sliced
40 g (1½ oz) butter
1 large onion, thinly sliced
2 cloves garlic, crushed
175 g (6 oz) mushrooms, sliced
20 ml (4 teaspoons) paprika
10 ml (2 teaspoons) mustard
30 ml (2 tablespoons) tomato purée
150 ml (¼ pint) chicken stock
salt and freshly ground black pepper
150 ml (¼ pint) soured cream
15 ml (1 tablespoon) chopped parsley

Heat the contact grill to High.

Melt the butter in the baking dish and fry the meat for about 2 minutes on each side. Remove the meat temporarily, and fry the onion and garlic for 1 — 2 minutes. Add the mushrooms and stir to coat them with butter.

Stir in the paprika, mustard and tomato purée and gradually pour on the stock. Bring the sauce to the boil, season with salt and pepper and return the meat.

Cover the dish with foil, cook between the grill plates for 10 minutes. Lower the heat to Medium and cook for 10 minutes more, or until the pork is tender. Stir in the soured cream and allow just to reheat. Serve garnished with the parsley.

Noodles make a very good accompaniment.

PORK CHOPS WITH NORWICH CREAM

15 ml (1 tablespoon) vegetable oil
4 pork chops
salt and freshly ground black pepper
150 ml (¼ pint) chicken stock
150 ml (¼ pint) white wine, or dry cider
60 ml (4 tablespoons) wholegrain mustard
150 ml (¼ pint) double cream
1 dessert apple, cored and sliced, to garnish
15 ml (1 tablespoon) lemon juice

Heat the contact grill to High.

Heat the oil in the baking dish. Snip the fat round the chops to prevent them from curling and brown them in the dish for about 2 minutes on each side. Remove the chops from the dish and season them with salt and pepper. Pour on the stock and wine or cider. Stir in the mustard. Return the chops to the pan, cover with foil and cook between the grill plates for about 20 minutes, or until they are thoroughly cooked.

Transfer the chops to a heated serving dish. Stir the cream into the sauce and add more salt and pepper if needed. Pour the sauce over the meat and garnish with the apple slices tossed in lemon juice.

HONEYED SPARE RIBS

900 g (2 lb) spare ribs of pork (ask the butcher for 'American' cut)
1 medium-sized onion, chopped
30 ml (2 tablespoons) clear honey
75 ml (5 tablespoons) tomato purée
30 ml (2 tablespoons) soy sauce
45 ml (3 tablespoons) red wine vinegar

150 ml (¼ pint) beef stock
a large pinch of cayenne
salt and freshly ground black pepper

Heat the contact grill to High.

Put the pork ribs in the baking dish and cook between the grill plates for 15 minutes. This drives off much of the fat. Pour it off, leaving about 30 ml (2 tablespoons).

Mix all the remaining ingredients together, pour over the pork and cook for a further 15 minutes, basting the ribs occasionally.

Reduce the heat to Low and cook for about 10 minutes more. The ribs should be crisp and the sauce much reduced and syrupy. Serve with rice or noodles.

EGG AND BACON CAKE

8 back rashers of bacon
15 g (½ oz) butter
2 large tomatoes, quartered
10 ml (2 teaspoons) chopped chives
15 ml (1 tablespoon) flour
90 ml (6 tablespoons) milk
6 eggs
salt and freshly ground black pepper
5 ml (1 teaspoon) chopped parsley, to garnish

Heat the contact grill to High.

Cut the rinds from the bacon. Melt a little of the butter in an ovenproof dish about 15× 23 cm (6 × 9 in). Arrange the bacon rashers and tomato wedges in the dish, brush the tomatoes with the butter and sprinkle them with the chives. Cook between the grill plates for about 3 minutes, until the bacon is crisp. Remove the bacon and tomatoes from the dish and keep them warm.

Melt the remaining butter in the dish.

Put the flour in a bowl. Gradually pour on the milk, stirring, to make a smooth paste. Beat in the eggs.

Pour the egg mixture into the dish, stir well and cook between the grill plates for about 4 minutes until the egg is just set. Remove from the heat at once. Arrange the bacon rashers and tomato in a pattern on top of the egg and return to the grill for a few moments. Garnish with the parsley. Serve very hot.

PAPRIKA SAUSAGES

450 g (1 lb) pork sausages
45 ml (3 tablespoons) vegetable oil
1 medium-sized onion, sliced
1 garlic clove, crushed
1 green pepper, de-seeded and sliced
1 red pepper, de-seeded and sliced
15 ml (1 tablespoon) paprika
salt and freshly ground black pepper
2.5 ml (½ teaspoon) dried oregano
400 g (14 oz) can tomatoes
225 g (8 oz) potatoes, peeled, cooked and thickly sliced
150 ml (¼ pint) soured cream
15 ml (1 tablespoon) chopped parsley, to garnish

Heat the contact grill to High.

Put the sausages in the baking dish and cook, between the grill plates, for about 15 minutes, until they are cooked through. Remove them and set aside.

Heat the oil in the baking dish and fry the onions and garlic for 1 minute. Add the pepper strips, stir and cook for 1 minute more.

Stir in the paprika, salt and pepper, herb and tomatoes

and stir well. Cover the dish with foil and cook between the grill plates for 5 minutes. Add the potatoes and sausages and cover the dish again. Reduce the heat to Medium and cook for 5 minutes. Stir in the soured cream and cook, uncovered, until it is just heated through.

Serve garnished with parsley.

BANGING-THE-DRUM CHICKEN

8 chicken drumsticks
15 g (½ oz) flour
salt and freshly ground black pepper
45 ml (3 tablespoons) vegetable oil
1 large onion, sliced
1 garlic clove, crushed
100 g (4 oz) gammon, cut into matchstick strips
300 ml (½ pint) chicken stock
grated rind and juice of 1 orange
15 ml (1 tablespoon) tomato purée
30 ml (2 tablespoons) Worcestershire sauce
50 g (2 oz) seedless raisins
salt and freshly ground black pepper
1 orange, thinly sliced, to garnish

Heat the contact grill to High.

Toss the chicken drumsticks in the flour seasoned with salt and pepper. Melt the oil in the baking dish and fry the chicken over a grill plate for 5 minutes, turning once. Add the onion and garlic, stir and fry for 2 minutes.

Add all the remaining ingredients except the orange slices. Stir well and cook between the grill plates for 15 — 20 minutes, until the chicken is tender. Garnish with the orange slices.

DAIRY CHICKEN

    4 chicken breasts, skinned
    15 ml (1 tablespoon) flour
    salt and freshly ground black pepper
    40 g (1½ oz) butter
    100 g (4 oz) mushrooms, sliced
    150 ml (¼ pint) dry cider
    15 ml (1 tablespoon) sweet sherry (optional)
    175 g (6 oz) Gruyère cheese, or similar, sliced
    15 ml (1 tablespoon) blanched almonds

Heat the contact grill to High.

Toss the chicken breasts in the flour well seasoned with salt and pepper. Melt the butter in the baking dish and fry the chicken for 2 minutes on each side. Remove the chicken temporarily and turn the mushrooms in the fat remaining in the dish, just for 1 minute.

Pour the cider and sweet sherry, if you like, into the dish, bring to the boil and boil for 2 minutes — the sauce should be slightly syrupy. Return the chicken to its rightful place, stir well and cover the dish with foil. Cook between the grill plates for 15 minutes, or until the chicken is cooked. Pierce it with a skewer or sharp knife to test.

Remove the foil. Arrange the chicken breasts neatly in an ovenproof dish with the mushrooms and sauce around them. Cover them with the cheese slices. Return to the closed grill for 2 minutes, scatter on the almonds and grill for 2 minutes more.

RED-BAKED CHICKEN

Tandoori style, steeped in the flavour of aromatic spices.

    4 chicken joints, skinned
    50 g (2 oz) butter
    15 −30 ml (1 − 2 tablespoons) paprika

For the marinade
   300 ml (½ pint) plain yoghurt
   5 ml (1 teaspoon) salt
   5 ml (1 teaspoon) turmeric
   5 ml (1 teaspoon) curry powder (mild or hot, to taste)
   15 ml (1 tablespoon) tomato purée
   juice of ½ lemon

Mix together all the marinade ingredients and spoon over the chicken joints in the baking dish. Cover with foil and leave in the refrigerator to marinate all day or overnight.

Heat the contact grill to High.

Melt the butter, pour it over the chicken and stir to blend it into the spiced yoghurt mixture. Cover the dish with foil again. Cook between the grill plates for 20 − 25 minutes, until the chicken is cooked. Pour off the sauce and serve it separately.

Sprinkle the chicken joints with paprika. Using the back of a spoon, rub the spice well into the flesh. Return the dish to the grill and cook for a further 5 minutes.

While you are dishing up the chicken you can cook poppadoms on the heated grill plates. Brush them with oil and grill until they are crisp.

Serve the chicken with rice and side dishes such as sliced onion and green pepper rings, bananas and desiccated coconut.

SESAME CHICKEN

   4 chicken joints
   25 g (1 oz) flour
   25 g (1 oz) sesame seeds
   salt and freshly ground black pepper
   60 ml (4 tablespoons) vegetable oil
   50 g (2 oz) blanched almonds

   8 spring onions, trimmed and cut into 7.5 cm (3 in)
      lengths
   60 ml (4 tablespoons) soy sauce
   75 ml (5 tablespoons) chicken stock
   1 garlic clove, chopped

Heat the contact grill to High.

Skin and halve the chicken joints so that you have 8 serving pieces. Mix together the flour, sesame seeds, salt and pepper and toss the chicken pieces to coat them thoroughly.

Heat the oil in the baking dish and fry the chicken and almonds, turning them frequently, for 3 — 4 minutes, until they are evenly brown. Add the spring onions, soy sauce, stock and garlic and stir thoroughly.

Cover the dish with foil and cook for 10 minutes. Lower the heat to Medium and cook for a further 5 minutes, or until the chicken is tender. Pierce it at the thickest part with a skewer or sharp knife to test.

Serve with rice and — if you like the idea — grilled fresh or canned peaches. These could cook on the already-heated grill while you are transferring the chicken to a serving dish.

PHEASANT MUSCAT

A delicious dinner party dish — made in just over half an hour.

   1 young pheasant, halved
   40 g (1½ oz) butter
   150 ml (¼ pint) unsweetened apple juice (the cloudy type
      is best)
   90 ml (6 tablespoons) soured cream
   salt and freshly ground black pepper
   30 ml (2 tablespoons) Calvados, if available, or brandy
   175 g (6 oz) seedless white grapes
   12 walnut halves, to garnish

Heat the contact grill to High.

Check that the pheasant halves fit in the pan and between the grill plates. If they do not, cut each one into two joints, giving four serving-sized pieces.

Melt the butter in the baking dish and fry the pheasant, turning it over to brown it on both sides, for about 4 minutes. Pour on the apple juice, stir in the soured cream and season with salt and pepper. Cover with foil and cook between the grill plates for 10 minutes. Lower the heat to Medium and stir in the Calvados or brandy and the grapes. Cover again and cook for a further 15 – 20 minutes, until the pheasant is tender. Test by piercing with a skewer or sharp knife. Taste the sauce and add more salt and pepper, or a pinch of sugar if needed. Transfer the pheasant to a serving dish, cover with the sauce and garnish with walnut halves.

As an alternative
Cook four pieces of chicken this way and — especially if you add the Calvados — they almost taste like pheasant!

VINEYARD RABBIT

Rabbit in a rich red wine sauce slightly sweetened by the dried fruit. You can also cook chicken joints in the same way.

   25 g (1 oz) flour
   2.5 ml (½ teaspoon) dried mixed herbs
   salt and freshly ground black pepper
   4 rabbit joints
   50 g (2 oz) butter
   1 medium-sized onion, sliced
   150 ml (¼ pint) red wine
   50 g (2 oz) seedless raisins
   30 ml (2 tablespoons) orange juice

Heat the contact grill to High.

Mix together the flour, herbs, salt and pepper and toss the rabbit joints to coat them thoroughly. Heat the butter in the baking dish and fry the onion and rabbit joints, turning them once, for about 4 minutes. Add the wine, raisins and orange juice.

Cover the dish with foil and cook between the grill plates for 10 minutes. Lower the heat to Medium and cook for a further 20 — 25 minutes, until the rabbit is tender. (The time depends on the type of rabbit and the size of the pieces.) Taste the sauce and add more salt and pepper if needed.

RABBIT JUNIPER

    4 rabbit joints
    25 g (1 oz) butter
    4 rashers streaky bacon, de-rinded and cut in squares
    15 g (1 oz) flour
    150 ml (¼ pint) chicken stock
    10 ml (2 teaspoons) French mustard
    60 ml (4 tablespoons) double cream
    15 ml (1 tablespoon) chopped parsley, for garnish

For the marinade
    150 ml (¼ pint) dry cider
    15 ml (1 tablespoon) vegetable oil
    1 medium-sized onion, sliced
    2 bay leaves
    salt and freshly ground black pepper
    2.5 ml (½ teaspoon) dried oregano
    2.5 ml (½ teaspoon) dried rosemary, crumbled

Put all the marinade ingredients into a small pan and bring them to the boil. Leave to cool, then tip the marinade into a large plastic bag, add the rabbit and tie the top. Leave in the refrigerator all day or overnight, turning once or twice if you can. Remove the rabbit, and pat the pieces dry with kitchen paper. Reserve the marinade.

Heat the contact grill to High.

Melt the butter in the baking dish and fry the rabbit pieces, turning them to brown them evenly, and the bacon for about 4 minutes. Stir in the flour and gradually pour on the stock, still stirring. (If yours is a small baking dish it might be easier to remove the rabbit while you do this.) Stir in the marinade and the mustard.

Cover the dish with foil. Cook between the grill plates for 15 minutes. Lower the heat to Medium and cook for a further 15 minutes, or until the rabbit is really tender. Remove the rabbit to a heated serving dish, stir the cream into the sauce and allow it just to heat. Pour the sauce over the rabbit and garnish with the parsley.

There might be room to cook vegetables in the sauce at the same time. Add small potatoes and baby carrots when the rabbit has been cooking in the sauce for 5 minutes.

BACON AND HERB ROLLS

Once you discover how quickly you can cook suet pastry on the contact grill, and what a delicate texture it has, you can ring the changes with minced meat, flaked fish, cheese or vegetables.

    100 g (4 oz) self-raising flour
    a pinch of salt
    a pinch of mixed dried herbs
    100 g (4 oz) shredded suet
    about 75 ml (5 tablespoons) water
    4 rashers collar or back bacon, de-rinded
    15 ml (1 tablespoon) chopped parsley
    1 small onion, finely chopped
    freshly ground black pepper

Heat the contact grill to High.

Cut a piece of foil about 25 × 40 cm (10 × 16 in) and grease it.

Stir together the flour, salt, dried herbs and suet and mix to a firm dough with the water. Roll out the pastry on a lightly-floured board.

Place the bacon rashers on the pastry and sprinkle them with the parsley, onion and pepper.

Do not roll up the pastry, roly-poly style — there isn't the height for that. Fold over one third, from the bottom, then the other third, from the top, to make a three-layer 'envelope'. Press together the edges and seal them.

Wrap the pastry, not too tightly, in the foil and double-seal the edges. Place in the baking dish. Cook between the grill plates for about 23 — 25 minutes. The pastry should be golden brown, and as light as a feather.

Leeks and new potatoes and a parsley sauce are my favourite accompaniments.

PORK AND APPLE PIE

This is just one example of a double-crust meat pie, made in a fraction of what we used to consider the 'normal' time. If you use cubed meat, rather than minced, pre-cook it in the baking dish.

 450 g (1 lb) shortcrust pastry
 550 g (1¼ lb) lean minced pork
 1 medium-sized onion, grated
 4 rashers lean bacon, de-rinded and finely chopped
 15 ml (1 tablespoon) chopped sage, or 5 ml (1 teaspoon)
  dried sage
 45 ml (3 tablespoons) sweet cider
 salt and freshly ground black pepper
 3 cooking apples, peeled, cored and thinly sliced
 40 g (1½ oz) mustard butter (page 50)
 milk, for brushing

Heat the contact grill to High. Grease the baking dish.

Divide the pastry dough in two and roll out each half to fit the dish. Lay the first piece of pastry in the dish.

Mix together the pork, onion, bacon, sage and cider and season with salt and pepper. Arrange half the apple slices to cover the pastry. Spread the meat mixture over and cover with the remaining apples. Flake the butter over the fruit. Lay the second piece of pastry on top. Re-roll any trimmings very thinly and cut them into leaves. Brush the pastry with milk, arrange a pattern of leaves and brush them.

Cover the dish with foil. Cook between the grill plates for 20 minutes — serve hot or cold.

This quantity fills a baking dish 18.5 × 30 cm (7½ × 12 in). Reduce the ingredient amounts proportionately if yours is smaller.
Serves 6

LIVER WITH APPLES AND SAGE

    450 g (1lb) lamb's liver, thinly sliced
    15 ml (1 tablespoon) flour
    2.5 ml (½ teaspoon) dried oregano
    salt and freshly ground black pepper
    15 g (½ oz) butter
    15 ml (1 tablespoon) vegetable oil
    2 dessert apples, cored and sliced
    6 whole sage leaves
    90 ml (6 tablespoons) chicken stock
    15 ml (1 tablespoon) dry sherry
    5 ml (1 teaspoon) lemon juice
    a pinch of sugar

Heat the contact grill to High.

Toss the liver slices in the flour seasoned with the oregano, salt and pepper.

Heat the butter and oil in the baking dish and fry the apple slices, turning them once, until they are brown – about 2 minutes. Remove the apples with a draining spoon.

Fry the liver slices in the oil remaining in the dish for 2 minutes on each side. Add the sage leaves, close the lid and cook the liver for a further 3 – 4 minutes, depending on how 'pink' you like it to be.

Pour on the stock, sherry and lemon juice, add the sugar and stir well. Cook, with the lid closed, for 2 minutes. Taste the sauce and add more salt and pepper if necessary. Remove the sage leaves.

Serve the liver garnished with the apple slices.

LIVER IN ONION SAUCE

   40 g (1½ oz) butter
   225 g (8 oz) onions, sliced
   40 g (1½ oz) flour
   425 ml (¾ pint) beef stock
   30 ml (2 tablespoons) tomato purée
   2.5 ml (½ teaspoon) dried marjoram
   10 ml (2 teaspoons) Worcestershire sauce
   salt and freshly ground black pepper
   450 g (1 lb) lamb's liver, cut into 12 mm (½ in) strips
   25 g (1 oz) stuffed olives, sliced

Heat the contact grill to High.

Melt the butter in the baking dish. Fry the onions for about 5 minutes, stirring occasionally, until they are well browned – the success of the dish depends on the onions being browned but not, of course, burned.

Stir in the flour to make a paste and gradually pour on the stock. Stir in the tomato purée, marjoram and sauce and season with salt and pepper. Cover the dish with foil and cook between the grill plates for 10 minutes to thicken the sauce.

Now introduce the liver to the sauce. Cover the pan again

and cook for 5 — 6 minutes, or until the liver is as 'done' as you like it. Stir in the olives.

HALIBUT OR COD STEAKS WITH BARBECUE SAUCE

    50 g (2 oz) butter
    4 halibut or cod steaks
    salt and freshly ground black pepper
    1 large onion, sliced
    1 red pepper, trimmed and finely chopped
    1 green pepper, trimmed and finely chopped
    2 garlic cloves, crushed
    30 ml (2 tablespoons) tomato purée
    15 ml (1 tablespoon) barbecue sauce, bought or see page 52
    a pinch of cayenne
    30 ml (2 tablespoons) water

Heat the contact grill to High.

Melt half the butter in the baking dish. Season the fish on both sides with salt and pepper and fry, between the grill plates, for 5 minutes, turning the fish once. Remove the fish to a plate while you make the sauce.

Melt the remaining butter in the dish and fry the onion, peppers and garlic for 2 minutes on the open grill. Stir in the tomato purée, barbecue sauce, cayenne and water, season with salt and pepper and cook for about 3 minutes.

Cut four pieces of foil each about 30 cm (12 in) square and grease them. Arrange a piece of fish in the centre of each. Divide the barbecue sauce between them. Fold up the foil to make neat, moisture-proof parcels.

Wash and dry the baking dish, arrange the parcels and cook them between the grill plates for 10 minutes.

Serve with rice and a green salad.

COD IN ORANGE SAUCE

4 cod steaks
4 prunes, stoned (some need pre-soaking)
4 blanched almonds
15 ml (1 tablespoon) vegetable oil
150 ml (¼ pint) unsweetened orange juice
15 ml (1 tablespoon) chopped parsley
15 ml (1 tablespoon) lemon juice
salt and freshly ground black pepper
2 spring onions, finely chopped
100 g (4 oz) button mushrooms, sliced
5 ml (1 teaspoon) flour
15 g (½ oz) butter

Remove the central bone from the cod steaks. Fill each prune with an almond and push the prunes into the holes left in the fish. Arrange the fish steaks in the baking dish and add all the remaining ingredients except the flour and butter. Cover the dish with foil and leave to marinate at room temperature for at least 2 hours. This way the orange flavour will penetrate the fish.

Heat the contact grill to Medium.

Turn the pieces of fish in the sauce. Cover with foil again and cook between the grill plates for about 10 minutes, or until the fish is just cooked. Do not overcook it, or it will become tough.

Mix the flour and butter together to make a thick paste. Transfer the fish to a heated serving dish. Stir the butter paste with the sauce to thicken it. Taste and add more salt and pepper, if needed. Pour the sauce over the fish.

POACHED COD 'PRINTEMPS'

700 g (1½ lb) cod fillet, skinned and cut across into 5 cm (2 in) slices
50 g (2 oz) butter

1 medium-sized onion, sliced
2 small carrots, sliced
2 small leeks, sliced
salt and freshly ground black pepper
300 ml (½ pint) medium-sweet cider
5 ml (1 teaspoon) lemon juice
15 ml (1 tablespoon) flour
60 ml (4 tablespoons) single cream
parsley sprigs, to garnish

Heat the contact grill to High.

Melt half the butter in the baking dish. Add the onion, carrots and leeks and fry for about 4 minutes, stirring occasionally. Arrange the pieces of fish in a single layer over the vegetables, season with salt and pepper and pour on the cider and lemon juice.

Cover the dish with foil. Reduce the heat to Medium and cook, between the grill plates, for 10 — 12 minutes, until the fish is just firm.

Mix the flour and the remaining butter together. Using a draining spoon, or fish slice, transfer the vegetables and fish to a heated serving dish. Stir the flour and butter paste into the juices remaining in the pan. When the sauce has thickened, stir in the cream and allow just to heat through. Pour the sauce over the fish. Garnish with the parsley sprigs.

CRUNCHY-TOP FISH

700 g (1½ lb) haddock or other white fish fillets, skinned
2 medium-sized onions, sliced
4 large tomatoes, skinned and chopped
3 small courgettes, thinly sliced
125 ml (4 fl oz) dry cider
15 ml (1 tablespoon) chopped mint, or tarragon (or 5 ml (1 teaspoon) dried herb)
salt and freshly ground black pepper

For the topping

    75 g (3 oz) breadcrumbs

    50 g (2 oz) Cheddar cheese, grated

    50 g (2 oz) cottage cheese

Heat the contact grill to High.

    Grease the baking dish and arrange the fish fillets. Cover them with the onion, tomato and courgette slices, pour on the cider, add the herb and season with salt and pepper. Cover the dish with foil and cook, between the grill plates, for 10 minutes.

    While the fish is cooking, mix together the breadcrumbs and cheeses for the topping.

    Remove the foil, sprinkle on the topping and cook for a further 5 minutes, or until the topping is crisp and brown.

ORIENT EXPRESS TROUT

    4 fresh trout, about 350g (12 oz) each, gutted and cleaned

    15 ml (1 tablespoon) cornflour

    45 ml (3 tablespoons) water

    45 ml (3 tablespoons) dry sherry

    15 ml (1 tablespoon) clear honey

    30 ml (2 tablespoons) soy sauce

    1 small onion, thinly sliced

    25 g (1 oz) fresh root ginger, thinly sliced

    100 g (4 oz) button mushrooms, sliced

    2 courgettes, thinly sliced

Arrange the trout in the baking dish. Put the cornflour in a small bowl, stir in the water to make a smooth paste, then mix with the sherry, honey and soy sauce. Pour this sauce over the trout and spoon it into the cavities. Add the onion and ginger. Cover the dish with foil and leave to marinate for at least 2 hours.

    Heat the contact grill to Medium.

Scatter the mushroom and courgette slices over the trout and spoon the sauce over them. Cover with foil again and cook between the grill plates for about 12 − 15 minutes, or until the trout are just cooked, turning the fish once.

Serve the trout on a bed of rice.

HONEYED MACKEREL

4 small mackerel
50 g (2 oz) breadcrumbs
50 g (2 oz) dried apricots, chopped
10 ml (2 teaspoons) chopped mint, or 5 ml (1 teaspoon) dried mint
30 ml (2 tablespoons) clear honey
salt and freshly ground black pepper
150 ml (¼ pint) dry cider
40 g (1½ oz) butter
30 ml (2 tablespoons) double cream
15 ml (1 tablespoon) chopped parsley, to garnish

Heat the contact grill to High.

Gut and clean the mackerel and remove the heads. Slit down the belly and cut away the backbones. Wash thoroughly.

Mix together the breadcrumbs, apricots, mint and honey and season the filling with salt and pepper. Divide the filling between the fish.

Grease the baking dish, arrange the fish, pour over the cider and flake on the butter. Cover the dish with foil and cook, between the grill plates, for 5 minutes. Lower the heat to Medium and cook for about 10 minutes more, or until the fish is just cooked.

Transfer the fish to a heated serving dish. Stir the cream into the sauce and just heat through. Taste the sauce and add more salt and pepper if needed. Pour over the fish and sprinkle with the parsley.

BAKED MACKEREL

8 mackerel fillets, skinned
1 small onion, finely chopped
30 ml (2 tablespoons) chopped parsley
grated rind and juice of 1 lemon
grated rind and juice of ½ orange
15 ml (1 tablespoon) tomato purée
freshly ground black pepper

Arrange the mackerel fillets in the baking dish. Mix together the remaining ingredients, pour them over the fish and cover the dish with foil. Leave to marinate for at least 2 hours.

Heat the contact grill to Medium. Baste the fish with the marinade and cook, uncovered, between the grill plates for 10 minutes.

SOUSED HERRING

4 small herrings, about 275 g (10 oz) each, gutted and cleaned
1 medium-sized onion, sliced
1 medium-sized carrot, sliced
1 lemon, sliced
1 dried red chilli, halved
2 bay leaves
8 — 10 black peppercorns
rock or sea salt
15 ml (1 tablespoon) capers
150 ml (¼ pint) dry white wine, or dry cider

Heat the contact grill to High.

Arrange the fish head-to-tail in the baking dish, scatter the vegetables and flavourings over them and pour on the wine or cider. Cover the dish with foil and cook between the grill plates for 5 minutes. Reduce the heat to Low and cook for about 20 − 25 minutes, or until the fish is tender. Test by piercing with a skewer or sharp knife.

Leave the fish to cool in the dish, then chill them in the refrigerator. Eat them cold, within 3 days.

ABERDEEN WHITING

Short of plain grilling, this must be the simplest-ever way of cooking fish deliciously.

    4 small whiting, gutted and cleaned
    15 ml (1 tablespoon) flour
    50 g (2 oz) butter
    30 ml (2 tablespoons) chopped parsley
    2 spring onions, finely chopped
    150 ml (¼ pint) single cream
    salt and freshly ground black pepper
    1 lemon, quartered, to garnish

Heat the contact grill to Medium.

Wash and thoroughly dry the fish and coat them in the flour. Pat it on firmly. Melt the butter in the baking dish and arrange the fish. Spoon the butter over them and cook them between the grill plates for about 4 minutes on each side.

Meanwhile, mix together the parsley, onion and cream and season the sauce with salt and pepper. Pour the sauce over the fish and cook for 5 minutes more. Carefully lift the fish on to a heated serving dish, pour on the sauce and garnish with the lemon wedges.

WHITING ROLLIES

    8 whiting fillets, skinned
    25 g (1 oz) butter, melted
    4 large tomatoes, halved

For the filling
   50 g (2 oz) butter, melted
   40 g (1½ oz) breadcrumbs
   25 g (1 oz) chopped walnuts
   15 ml (1 tablespoon) chopped parsley
   15 ml (1 tablespoon) chopped mint
   grated rind and juice of 1 lemon
   salt and freshly ground black pepper

Heat the contact grill to Medium.

Mix together the ingredients for the filling. Arrange the fish fillets, skinned side down, on the table. Divide the filling between them, spread it evenly and roll up the fillets like mini Swiss rolls. Secure each one with a wooden cocktail stick.

Grease the baking dish, arrange the fish rolls and tomatoes in it, season them with salt and pepper and dribble the butter over them. Grill for about 10 minutes, or until the whiting are just firm. Remove the cocktail sticks before serving.

For a change
Use plaice fillets, filled and rolled in the same way.

5   Vegetables, Cheese and Eggs

Carrot and sweetcorn crumble, orange and golden-delicious; a cool, clear salad of grilled green peppers; potatoes cooked in their jackets, with soured cream and paprika, parcelled up with bags of flavour, or just plain roast; slices of Spanish omelette peppered with colourful vegetables; cheese pudding pungent with herbs and spices; and eggs lightly baked a-top a bed of mushrooms; vegetable dishes can be very good!

This chapter begins at the beginning, with basic ways to grill or parcel up one or several types of vegetable: the whys and wherefores of the two techniques, the preparation and the flavourings. Juggle your cooking times around, and you will find that, plain grilled or parcel-wrapped, vegetables can be cooked alongside meat, fish and other ingredients.

Kebabs of tender vegetables to pop into a piece of pitta, ratatouille, that fragrant Mediterranean medley to serve hot or (even better) chilled — there are plenty of recipes to show you how to blend flavours, build up texture contrasts and delight everyone round the table.

But don't stop there. Vegetables can replace meat and fish (some think even more deliciously) in crumbles, gratins and baked puddings. Carrot crumble and mushroom and barley bake are high on my list of favourites.

Vegetables can also make such scrumptious containers for savoury mixes of rice, herbs, dried fruits, nuts, cheese, little left-over tasty morsels. This way, filled vegetables can be served as an opening course Italian-restaurant style, or with new potatoes, noodles or rice as a main dish.

Eggs and cheese have lots of possibilities on the contact grill. Baked eggs sitting on vegetables, creamy cheese pudding with a colourful topping, even a roulade — a very grand kind of cheese roll; these and many more are all here.

GRILLED VEGETABLES

Quick-cook vegetables — which in general means those with a high moisture content — cook perfectly under the grill, brushed with oil or butter, flavoured with herbs or spices, made extra tasty with toasted cheese — as you will.

Mushrooms, tomatoes, red or green peppers, aubergines and courgettes are all ideal candidates for simply grilling.

Preparation
Wipe mushrooms and trim the stalks, halve tomatoes crossways, halve red or green peppers and discard the seeds and white pith, halve aubergines and very young courgettes lengthways — older specimens can be sliced. Sprinkle aubergines and courgettes with cooking salt, drain them in a colander for at least 30 minutes, then wash under cold, running water, drain and dry thoroughly.

Oil
Use your favourite vegetable oil — olive, corn, sunflower, walnut — or a herb-flavoured one which you can make by just infusing sprigs of rosemary, bay or tarragon in the bottle. Or crush a few spice seeds — black, green or white peppercorns, fennel, coriander or allspice — or a clove of garlic into the oil before you start cooking.

Butter
Use melted unsalted butter, or better still one of the flavoured butters (pages 49–51) to give a real 'lift' to your

vegetables. Basil butter with tomatoes, paprika butter with mushrooms, orange with aubergines, there's a whole new range of flavours around the corner!

Cooking

Arrange the vegetables in the baking dish or directly on to the lower grill plate, first brushed with oil or melted butter. Season the vegetables with freshly ground black pepper and a pinch of ground spice if you wish, then brush them with the oil or butter. Cook between the grill plates with the appliance pre-heated to High. Grill mushrooms for about 2 minutes, tomato or pepper halves about 3 minutes, aubergine or courgette halves about 4 − 5 minutes, slices about 2 minutes.

Toppings

You can add tasty toppings that give extra flavours and a good contrast of textures − a welcome crunchiness marrying up with the soft vegetables. Stir breadcrumbs, lightly crushed cream crackers or bran flakes or rolled porridge oats into melted butter and ring the changes with chopped fresh herbs or grated cheese. Grill the vegetables first, then press the topping on firmly and grill for 3 minutes more to crisp up.

PARCELLED VEGETABLES

All the 'toughies', like potatoes, carrots and swedes, *can* be grilled, but it's a chancy business to cook them to perfection without their drying out. (The secret is to boil or steam them until they are about three-quarters tender, then to season, brush and grill them.) But why bother? Root vegetables as well as all the 'softies' (marrow and mushrooms, for example) cook like a dream in puffy foil parcels.

Preparation

Prepare the vegetables in the usual way, sliced, diced, whole
or halved according to age and size. Carrots, whole, halved,
diced, sliced; celeriac, thinly sliced or finely diced; celery
heart whole if very small, or halved or quartered; courgettes
whole or halved; Florentine fennel, halved or quartered;
leeks whole if very small, or sliced; marrow (seeded if old),
cut into rings or cubes; mushrooms, whole or sliced; onions
whole, halved or sliced; potatoes in or out of their skins, and
whole if they are young and small; swedes and turnips, diced
or sliced. Cut the vegetables into even-sized pieces and — the
joy of this technique — mix and match them, several types
together. Courgettes, mushrooms and tomato slices;
potatoes and carrots (see sample recipe, page 93); swedes,
turnips, onions and tomatoes; celery, marrow and mushrooms — it's a permutation puzzle.

Cut the longer-cooking 'toughies' into the smallest pieces
to mix with whole or halved short-time ones, and they'll all
be tender and tasty together.

Grease a piece of foil large enough to enclose the vegetables with secure, double seams into slightly puffy parcels —
you need space for the head of steam that cooks them.

Sprinkle the vegetables with herbs and flakes of butter or
with a flavoured butter and season them well with pepper
and salt and, if you like, a hint of spice. For a creaminess that
is delicious, add plain yoghurt, single, double or soured
cream; try, for example, yoghurt, curry powder and chopped
parsley with courgettes, double cream and mint butter with
peas.

Cook the parcels between the grill plates, the appliance set
on High, until they are tender. I am sorry to be vague, but the
timing *does* depend on the age and type of vegetable and the
size you choose. Thirty minutes is a good average for root
vegetables, 15 minutes for soft ones.

MINTY POTATOES

New potatoes and carrots aren't just for boiling; here they're for foiling.

    450 g (1 lb) new potatoes, scraped
    350 g (12 oz) baby carrots, scraped
    30 ml (2 tablespoons) chopped mint
    salt and freshly ground black pepper
    75 g (3 oz) butter
    15 ml (1 tablespoon) chopped chives, to garnish

Heat the contact grill to High.

Cut a double thickness of foil about 61 cm (24 in) square and grease it well. Arrange the potatoes and carrots in the centre, sprinkle on the mint and season with salt and pepper. Cut the butter into small pieces over the vegetables. Fold over and seal the foil, making a slightly 'puffy' rather than a tight parcel.

Put the parcel in the baking dish and cook between the grill plates for about 30 minutes, or until the vegetables are just tender. Turn them into a heated serving dish and garnish with the chives.

PAPRIKA POTATOES

    900 g (2 lb) potatoes
    salt
    30 ml (2 tablespoons) vegetable oil
    1 medium-sized onion, sliced
    1 garlic clove, crushed
    1 green pepper, de-seeded and finely chopped
    2 medium-sized tomatoes, skinned and chopped
    15 ml (1 tablespoon) paprika
    1.5 ml (¼ teaspoon) caraway seeds (optional)
    freshly ground black pepper
    425 ml (¾ pint) chicken stock

125 ml (4 fl oz) soured cream
5 ml (1 teaspoon) chopped parsley, to garnish

Peel the potatoes and boil them in salted water for 7 minutes, to partly cook them. Drain and cut them into 6 mm (¼ in) slices.

Heat the contact grill to High.

Heat the oil in the baking dish and fry the onion, garlic and green pepper for 2 minutes, stirring. Add the tomato and cook for 1 minute. Stir in the paprika and caraway seeds if you like them and season with salt and pepper. Stir in the chicken stock, bring the sauce to the boil and add the potatoes.

Cover the dish with greased foil and cook, between the grill plates, for 15 minutes. Remove the foil, spread the soured cream over and return to cook for 3 minutes. Serve hot, garnished with the parsley.

It should be possible to cut the potatoes in slices, like a cake.

Serves 6

SPRING GARDEN POTATOES

450 g (1 lb) potatoes, peeled and sliced
1 large onion, sliced
salt and freshly ground black pepper
a pinch of grated nutmeg
15 ml (1 tablespoon) chopped parsley
150 ml (¼ pint) milk, or single cream

Heat the contact grill to High.

Grease the baking dish and make layers of the potato slices and onion, seasoning each one with salt, pepper, nutmeg and parsley, finishing with potatoes. Pour on the milk or cream.

Cover with greased foil and cook, between the grill plates, for 25 − 30 minutes, or until the potato topping is deep, dark brown. Serve hot.

POTATO BROWNIE

450 g (1 lb) potatoes, peeled
salt
100 g (4 oz) butter
30 ml (2 tablespoons) milk
freshly ground black pepper
a pinch of grated nutmeg
450 g (1 lb) onions, sliced

Cook the potatoes in boiling, salted water until they are tender. Drain them and mash them with 25 g (1 oz) of the butter and milk. Beat until creamy, then season with pepper and nutmeg.

Heat the contact grill to High.

Melt 50 g (2 oz) of the remaining butter in the baking dish and fry the onions between the grill plates, stirring frequently, until they are translucent but not brown. Turn the onions into the mashed potato and mix well.

Melt the remaining butter in the dish. Tip in the potato mixture and smooth the top. Cook between the grill plates for about 10 minutes, until the top is crisp and dark brown.

ROAST POTATOES

These could be the crispiest you ever cooked.

700 g (1½ lb) medium-sized potatoes, peeled
salt
75 g (3 oz) white vegetable fat or lard

Partly cook the potatoes in boiling, salted water for 5 — 6 minutes. Drain them and pat them dry.

Heat the contact grill to High.

Melt the fat in the baking dish, add the potatoes and cover with foil. Cook between the grill plates for 10 — 12 minutes, or until the potatoes are crispy, crunchy brown outside. They should then be soft and floury inside. Serve at once.

DINNER-JACKET POTATOES

    4 medium-sized potatoes, scrubbed
    vegetable oil, for brushing
    50 g (2 oz) butter
    100 g (4 oz) mushrooms, sliced
    salt and freshly ground black pepper
    50 g (2 oz) Cheddar cheese, grated
    1 egg
    15 ml (1 tablespoon) chopped parsley

Heat the contact grill to High.

Check the size of the potatoes — they must fit comfortably between the grill plates. Prick the skins and brush them with oil. Place them in the baking dish and cook them between the grill plates, turning them occasionally, for about 25 minutes, or until the potatoes are tender and the skins crispy brown. Remove from the grill.

Melt the butter in a pan on the grill plate, add the mushrooms and stir for 1 minute, then take the pan from the heat.

Cut the potatoes in half and scoop out the flesh into a bowl. Stir in the mushrooms and season with salt and pepper. Beat in the cheese, egg and parsley and spoon the mixture into the potato shells. Arrange them in the baking dish and cook between the grill plates for 5 — 7 minutes, or until the potato filling is well risen, light and delicious.

GRILLED PEPPER SALAD

The skin blackens alarmingly — but then you rub it off.

    3 green peppers
    3 red peppers
    45 ml (3 tablespoons) chopped parsley
    2 garlic cloves, crushed
    40 g (1½ oz) walnut halves

60 ml (4 tablespoons) olive oil
10 ml (2 teaspoons) lemon juice
salt and freshly ground black pepper

Heat the contact grill to High.

Cut off the stalks from the peppers, cut them in half and discard the seeds and pith. Arrange the peppers cut side down in the baking dish and cook them between the grill plates for about 4 minutes, until the skins are black. (In a small appliance, grill the peppers in two batches.) Quickly cool them in cold water, then drain and rub off the skins. Pat them dry.

Slice the peppers and toss them with the parsley, garlic and walnuts.

Pour the oil and lemon juice into the baking dish and bring it to the boil. Pour it over the pepper salad and mix thoroughly. Leave to cool.
Serves 4—6

VEGETABLE KEBABS

A spectacular way to serve a selection of vegetables as an accompaniment. Or, on a bed of rice, as a light meal.

8 small onions, skinned
4 small tomatoes, skinned
4 large courgettes, cut into 2.5 cm (1 in) slices
225 g (8 oz) small button mushrooms
2 bananas, quartered
4 bay leaves
45 ml (3 tablespoons) vegetable oil
1 garlic clove, crushed
15 ml (1 tablespoon) red wine vinegar
salt and freshly ground black pepper

Heat the contact grill to High.

Blanch the onions in boiling water for 3 minutes, to take away the 'raw' taste. Drain and dry them thoroughly. Divide the onions, tomatoes (halved if necessary), courgette slices, mushrooms, bananas and bay leaves between four skewers.

Mix together the oil, garlic and vinegar and season with salt and pepper. Brush the skewers with the sauce. Arrange them on the lower grill plate and grill them, between the two plates, for 2 minutes. Turn the skewers, brush them with the oil mixture again and continue grilling for about 3 minutes, or until all the vegetables are tender. Serve hot with pitta bread (page 196).

RATATOUILLE

A medley of summer vegetables with a distinctly Mediterranean flavour.

  60 ml (4 tablespoons) vegetable oil
  2 medium-sized onions, sliced
  1 green pepper, de-seeded and thinly sliced
  2 garlic cloves, crushed
  1 medium-sized aubergine, diced
  350 g (12 oz) courgettes, cut into 2.5 cm (1 in) slices
  350 g (12 oz) tomatoes, skinned and sliced
  10 ml (2 teaspoons) sugar
  salt and freshly ground black pepper
  15 ml (1 tablespoon) chopped parsley
  5 ml (1 teaspoon) dried basil

Heat the contact grill to High.

Heat the oil in the baking dish and fry the onions, stirring, for 1 minute. Add the green pepper and garlic, stir and fry for 3 minutes more. Add the aubergine and courgettes, stir well and cover the dish with foil. Reduce the heat to Medium. Cook between the grill plates for 10 minutes. Add the tomatoes, sugar, salt, pepper and herbs, stir, cover again and cook for a further 10 — 12 minutes, until the vegetables are tender but not mushy.

Ratatouille is delicious served hot, to accompany meat and fish. To serve it with a grill, stand the baking dish, still covered with foil, on top of the appliance to keep warm while you grill the star attraction.

It is just as good cold, a perfect cook-ahead starter.

Serves 4 — 6

SWEET STUFFED AUBERGINES

4 medium-sized aubergines
salt
75 g (3 oz) long-grain rice
1 medium-sized onion, grated
225 ml (8 fl oz) chicken stock
40 g (1½ oz) raisins
40 g (1½ oz) sultanas
2 large tomatoes, skinned and sliced
40 g (1½ oz) blanched almonds, sliced
2.5 ml (½ teaspoon) ground coriander
a pinch of mixed spice
freshly ground black pepper
30 ml (2 tablespoons) chopped parsley
150 ml (¼ pint) tomato juice

Halve the aubergines along the length and, using a teaspoon, scoop out and discard the seeds. Then scoop out more of the flesh, to leave good firm 'walls'. Sprinkle the aubergine shells and the separate flesh with salt and leave them in a colander to drain for about 1 hour. Rinse under cold, running water, then drain and dry.

Heat the contact grill to Medium.

Put the rice and onion in the baking dish with 175 ml (6 fl oz) of the stock, bring to the boil, cover with foil and cook for about 12 − 15 minutes, until the rice has absorbed the stock. Add the raisins, sultanas, tomatoes, almonds and reserved aubergine flesh, season with the coriander, mixed spice, salt and pepper and stir in half the chopped parsley. Stir over the heat for 1 minute.

Fill the aubergine shells with the mixture, packing it well down. Arrange the aubergines in the rinsed baking dish, pour on the reserved chicken stock and the tomato juice and season with salt and pepper. Cover with greased foil and cook, between the grill plates, for about 15 minutes, until the aubergines are tender. Serve hot.

AUBERGINE GRATIN

Rich and filling, this dish needs nothing more than a salad and hot, crusty rolls.

> 1 large aubergine, about 350 g (12 oz)
> salt
> flour
> vegetable oil
> 225 g (8 oz) cottage cheese
> 3 eggs, beaten
> 50 g (2 oz) Gruyère cheese, grated
> freshly ground black pepper

Cut the top and bottom from the aubergine. Slice it thinly and put in a colander. Liberally sprinkle it with salt and leave for about 1 hour, to drain off some of the moisture. Rinse the aubergine slices under cold, running water, and pat them dry with kitchen paper. Toss them in flour to coat them thoroughly.

Heat the contact grill to High.

Heat about 60 ml (4 tablespoons) of oil in the baking dish and fry a few aubergine slices at a time, with the top grill plate closed, until they are golden brown. Remove the cooked aubergine with a slotted spoon and keep warm. Add more oil and fry the remainder. Take the dish from the heat.

Beat the cottage cheese into the eggs, stir in all but 30 ml (2 tablespoons) of the grated cheese and season with pepper.

Arrange a layer of aubergine in the dish, cover with some of the cheese mixture and make more layers, finishing with aubergines. Sprinkle on the grated cheese.

Cook between the grill plates for about 8 – 10 minutes, until the top is deep brown.
Serves 4 – 6

CUCUMBER BOATS

2 medium-sized cucumbers, peeled
salt
25 g (1 oz) butter
175 g (6 oz) mushrooms, chopped
25 g (1 oz) flour
150 ml (¼ pint) milk
15 ml (1 tablespoon) chopped parsley
freshly ground black pepper
a pinch of grated nutmeg
25 g (1 oz) Cheddar cheese, grated
1 hard-boiled egg, sliced, to garnish

Cut a thin slice from each end of the cucumbers. Cut them in half lengthways, and, using a teaspoon, scoop out the seeds. Cut each piece into three – you will now have 12 'cucumber boats'. Put them into a colander, sprinkle them with salt and leave them for 30 minutes to drain. This gets rid of some of the 'excess' moisture. Rinse and dry them.

Heat the contact grill to High. Grease the baking dish.

Melt the butter in a pan and fry the mushrooms, stirring once or twice, for 2 minutes. Stir in the flour, gradually pour on the milk and stir until the sauce boils. Stir in the parsley and season with salt and pepper and a pinch of nutmeg. Simmer for 2 minutes.

Arrange the cucumber pieces in the baking dish and spoon on the mushroom filling. Sprinkle on the cheese.

Cook between the grill plates for 8 – 10 minutes, until the cucumber is just tender. Garnish with the egg slices and serve hot.

MARROW RINGS

1 small marrow
50 g (2 oz) breadcrumbs
50 g (2oz) coarsely-grated nuts, e.g. almonds, brazils, walnuts
30 ml (2 tablespoons) chopped parsley
30 ml (2 tablespoons) vegetable oil
1 small onion, grated or finely chopped
50 g (2 oz) Wensleydale cheese, grated
grated rind and juice of ½ lemon
2 large tomatoes, skinned and chopped
1 small egg, beaten
salt and freshly ground black pepper

Heat the contact grill to High. Grease the baking dish.

Cut four 4 cm (1½ in) slices from the marrow. Peel it only if the skin is old and tough. Mix together all the remaining ingredients. Arrange the marrow slices in the dish and divide the filling between them, patting it firmly down.

Cover the dish with greased foil and cook, between the grill plates, for 15 – 20 minutes, until the marrow is just tender. Serve hot.

Tomato or onion sauce are good accompaniments.

ONIONS WITH A CHEESE TOPPER

An economical main dish to serve with rice and salad.

      4 large Spanish onions, skinned
      salt
      40 g (1½ oz) butter
      1 green pepper, de-seeded and finely chopped
      1 garlic clove, crushed
      100 g (4 oz) canned tomatoes, drained and chopped
      5 ml (1 teaspoon) dried oregano
      freshly ground black pepper

For the topping
      25 g (1 oz) rolled porridge oats
      25 g (1 oz) hazelnuts, coarsely grated or chopped
      40 g (1½ oz) Cheddar cheese, grated
      30 ml (2 tablespoons) soured cream
      salt and freshly ground black pepper

Heat the contact grill to High.

Blanch the onions by boiling them in salted water for 3 minutes. Drain them thoroughly. Scoop out the centres, leaving firm walls. Check the height of the onions by placing them in the baking dish between the grill plates. Cut a slice from the top if necessary, so that they fit.

Melt the butter in the baking dish and fry the pepper, garlic, tomatoes and chopped onion centres, stirring, for 2 minutes. Season with the oregano, salt and pepper. Divide this filling between the four onions, packing it down well.

Rinse the baking dish and arrange the onions.

Mix together the oats, nuts, cheese and soured cream for the topping, and season with salt and pepper. Spoon this mixture into the onions.

Cover the dish with greased foil and cook between the grill plates for about 10 — 15 minutes, until the onions are crisp and deep brown.

Serve hot.

SWEET AND SOUR ONIONS

A sparky way to serve onions, with roast or grilled poultry or meat.

8 medium-sized onions, skinned
salt
freshly ground black pepper
75 g (3 oz) soft light brown sugar
300 ml (½ pint) chicken stock
15 ml (1 tablespoon) cornflour
15 ml (1 tablespoon) red wine vinegar
5 ml (1 teaspoon) soy sauce
10 ml (2 teaspoons) chopped parsley, for garnish

Heat the contact grill to High.

Blanch the onions in boiling, salted water for 5 minutes, then drain them.

Arrange them in the baking dish, season them with salt and pepper and sprinkle on the sugar. Pour on the stock and cover with greased foil.

Cook, between the grill plates, for 15 minutes. Transfer the onions to a heated serving dish and keep warm. Mix the cornflour to a paste with the vinegar and soy sauce and stir into the juices in the pan. Bring to the boil, stir until the sauce thickens and pour over the onions. Garnish with the parsley and serve hot.

GREEN PEPPERS WITH NUTS AND RICE

A cook now, serve later cold dish.

4 green peppers
salt
30 ml (2 tablespoons) vegetable oil
1 medium-sized onion, chopped
1 garlic clove, crushed
75 g (3 oz) long-grain rice

225 ml (8 fl oz) tomato juice
50 g (2 oz) brazil nuts, coarsely chopped
15 ml (1 tablespoon) chopped parsley
5 ml (1 teaspoon) dried oregano
freshly ground black pepper
150 ml (¼ pint) chicken stock
15 ml (1 tablespoon) tomato purée

Heat the contact grill to High.

Cut the tops from the peppers, scrape out and discard the seeds and the white pith and blanch the peppers in boiling, salted water for 5 minutes. Drain them and cut them crossways in half. There will not be the height to leave them whole.

Heat the oil in the baking dish and fry the onion and garlic, stirring, for 1 minute. Stir in the rice to coat all the grains with oil. Pour on the tomato juice and stir well. Cover the dish with greased foil. Reduce the heat to Medium and cook, between the grill plates, for 10 minutes, or until the rice is tender. Stir in the nuts and herbs and season with salt and pepper. Divide the filling between the eight pepper halves.

Rinse the baking dish and arrange the peppers, lifting them carefully on a fish slice. Pour on the chicken stock and stir in the tomato purée, season with salt and pepper.

Cover the dish with foil again and cook, between the grill plates, for about 10 − 15 minutes, until the peppers are tender.

Remove from the heat and leave to cool in the dish, spooning the dressing over the peppers until it has been absorbed.

BROCCOLI BAKE

A meal in itself, for non-meat days.

450 g (1 lb) broccoli or calabrese
2 medium-sized carrots, diced

salt
2 spring onions, finely chopped
350 g (12 oz) cottage cheese
2 eggs, beaten
freshly ground black pepper

For the topping
100 g (4 oz) breadcrumbs
50 g (2 oz) Cheddar cheese, grated
25 g (1 oz) chopped walnuts
50 g (2 oz) butter, melted

Heat the contact grill to Medium.

Spread the breadcrumbs on the baking dish and toast them between the grill plates for about 2 minutes, stirring once or twice, until they are golden brown. Cool the crumbs and mix them with the cheese and walnuts. Set aside.

Break the broccoli into florets and cook with the carrots in boiling, salted water for 8 minutes. Drain thoroughly and toss on crumpled kitchen paper.

Mix the broccoli and carrots with the spring onions and cottage cheese, stir in the beaten eggs and season with salt and pepper.

Grease the baking dish and turn the vegetable mixture into it. Mix the crumbs with the melted butter and spread them on top. Cover with greased foil and cook between the grill plates for about 12 minutes, or until the egg and vegetable layer has set and the crumbly topping is well browned. Serve hot.

Serves 6

CARROT CRUMBLE

450 g (1 lb) carrots, diced
150 ml (¼ pint) chicken stock

100 g (4 oz) canned sweetcorn, drained
2.5 ml (½ teaspoon) ground coriander
5 ml (1 teaspoon) soft light brown sugar
15 g (½ oz) butter
salt and freshly ground black pepper

For the topping
50 g (2 oz) butter or margarine
100 g (4 oz) wholewheat flour
25 g (1 oz) wholewheat breadcrumbs
5 ml (1 teaspoon) sunflower seeds
2.5 ml (½ teaspoon) ground coriander

Cook the carrots in the stock until they are just tender. Mix them with the sweetcorn, coriander, sugar and butter and season with salt and pepper. Spread the mixture in a greased baking dish.

Heat the contact grill to High.

To make the topping, rub the butter or margarine into the flour, stir in the breadcrumbs, sunflower seeds and coriander and season with salt and pepper. Sprinkle the topping over the vegetable mixture.

Cook the crumble, between the grill plates, for about 15 minutes, or until the topping is crisp and brown.

For a change
Other combinations of seasonal or frozen vegetables offer endless possibilities — broad beans with carrots; peas and french beans with sweetcorn; celery and green peppers with tomatoes — it's fun to experiment.
Serves 4 as a main dish, 6 as an accompaniment

CARROT PUDDING

700 g (1½ lb) carrots, sliced
2 small onions, skinned
salt

75 g (3 oz) butter
50 g (2 oz) flour
300 ml (½ pint) milk
3 eggs, separated
freshly ground black pepper
25 g (1 oz) Cheddar cheese, grated

Cook the carrots and whole onions in boiling, salted water for about 10 minutes, or until they are tender. Drain the vegetables. Mash the carrots and finely chop the onions.

Heat the contact grill to High. Grease the baking dish.

Melt the butter in a pan, stir in the flour and gradually pour on the milk. Bring to the boil and simmer for 3 minutes. Remove from the heat, stir in the carrot and onion and beat in the egg yolks and pepper. Allow to cool.

Whisk the egg whites until they are stiff and fold them into the vegetable mixture. Turn into the baking dish, smooth the top and sprinkle with the cheese.

Cook between the grill plates for about 12 − 15 minutes, until the pudding is just set, but still light and fluffy. Serve hot.

A green vegetable such as spinach tossed in single cream, or broccoli spears, is a perfect partner. So is a green salad.

CAULIFLOWER CHEESE

1 large cauliflower, cut into florets
150 ml (¼ pint) chicken stock
75 g (3 oz) breadcrumbs
175 g (6 oz) Cheddar cheese, grated
75 g (3 oz) chopped walnuts
15 ml (1 tablespoon) flour
a pinch of grated nutmeg
salt and freshly ground black pepper
2 large tomatoes, sliced

Heat the contact grill to High.

Cook the cauliflower florets in the stock for 10 − 12 minutes, until the vegetable is soft. Purée with any remaining stock in a blender.

Mix the purée with the breadcrumbs, 100 g (4 oz) of the cheese, the walnuts and flour and season well with nutmeg, salt and pepper.

Grease the baking dish and pour in the cauliflower mixture. Smooth the top and arrange the tomato slices in a pattern. Sprinkle on the remaining cheese. Cook between the grill plates for 10 − 12 minutes, until the purée is set and the topping golden brown. Serve hot.

A crisp, cool green salad is an ideal partner.

BRAISED FENNEL

    4 large bulbs of fennel
    10 ml (2 teaspoons) lemon juice
    25 g (1 oz) butter
    150 ml (¼ pint) chicken stock
    salt and freshly ground black pepper
    10 ml (2 teaspoons) butter, softened
    10 ml (2 teaspoons) flour
    15 ml (1 tablespoon) chopped parsley, to garnish

Heat the contact grill to High.

Wash and trim the fennel, strip off the tough outer leaves and cut each bulb in half lengthways.

Arrange the fennel halves in the baking dish, add the lemon juice, butter and stock and season with salt and pepper. Put the dish on the grill plate and bring to simmering point. Cover with foil and cook between the grill plates for about 12 − 15 minutes.

Mix together the butter and flour to make a smooth paste and stir into the sauce until it thickens. Sprinkle on the parsley to garnish.

LEEK CROÛTON

Crunchy-topped leeks in a cheese sauce.

    40 g (1½ oz) butter
    700 g (1½ lb) leeks, cut into 2.5 cm (1 in) slices
    40 g (1½ oz) flour
    300 ml (½ pint) milk
    100 g (4 oz) Cheddar cheese, grated
    15 ml (1 tablespoon) chopped parsley
    salt and freshly ground black pepper
    4 slices bread, cut into 12 mm (½ in) cubes

Heat the contact grill to High.

Melt the butter in a pan on the grill plate and cook the leeks for 5 minutes, stirring occasionally. Stir in the flour and gradually pour on the milk, stirring until the sauce thickens. Add 75 g (3 oz) of the cheese and the parsley and season with salt and pepper.

Pour into the baking dish, sprinkle on the bread cubes, which make a nice crunchy topping, and then the remaining cheese.

Cook between the grill plates for 8 − 10 minutes, until the cheese is bubbling brown. Serve hot.

MUSHROOM AND BARLEY BAKE

A perfect food balance of vegetable and grain, high in vitamins and fibre.

    30 ml (2 tablespoons) vegetable oil
    2 large onions, sliced
    225 g (8 oz) mushrooms, sliced
    1 green pepper, de-seeded and sliced
    175 g (6 oz) pearl barley
    400 g (14 oz) canned tomatoes
    100 ml (3½ fl oz) chicken stock

  10 ml (2 teaspoons) chopped thyme
  salt and freshly ground black pepper
  15 ml (1 tablespoon) chopped parsley, for garnish

Heat the contact grill to High.

Heat the oil in the baking dish and fry the onions for 3 minutes. Add the mushrooms and pepper and stir well, before adding the pearl barley. Stir the grains in thoroughly, then tip in the tomatoes and stock. Season with the thyme, salt and pepper and cover the dish with foil.

Lower the heat to Medium and cook between the grill plates for about 30 minutes, or until the grains are soft — you will have to taste a few to be sure — and have absorbed most of the stock. Sprinkle on the parsley to garnish. Serve hot.

For a change
Keep the barley, onions and tomatoes, but substitute french beans, sweetcorn, carrots, peas for the other vegetables.

VEGETABLE CURRY

  225 g (8 oz) carrots, diced
  1 small cauliflower, cut into florets
  450 g (1 lb) potatoes, diced
  salt
  40 g (1½ oz) butter
  2 large onions, sliced
  10 ml (2 teaspoons) curry powder (mild or hot, to taste)
  15 ml (1 tablespoon) tomato purée
  150 ml (¼ pint) plain yoghurt
  100 g (4 oz) frozen peas, thawed

Heat the contact grill to High.

Partly cook the carrots, cauliflower and potatoes in boiling, salted water for 5 minutes. Strain the vegetables and reserve the stock.

Melt the butter in the baking dish and fry the onions, stirring occasionally, for 3 − 4 minutes. Stir in the curry powder and tomato purée and cook for 1 minute. Pour on 150 ml (¼ pint) of the vegetable stock and then the yoghurt. Season the sauce with salt.

Add all the vegetables (including the peas), stir carefully and cover the dish with foil. Cook between the grill plates for 10 minutes, until the vegetables are just tender. Serve hot.

In the time it takes to transfer the curry to a serving dish, and while the grill plates are hot, you can grill poppadoms (brush them first with oil) or pitta bread (page 196).

CHEESE PUDDING

50 g (2 oz) butter
1 small onion, chopped
50 g (2 oz) flour
300 ml (½ pint) milk
50 g (2 oz) Danish blue cheese
50 g (2 oz) Wensleydale cheese
4 eggs, separated
50 g (2 oz) breadcrumbs
30 ml (2 tablespoons) chopped parsley
2.5 ml (½ teaspoon) Worcestershire sauce
salt and freshly ground black pepper
1 green pepper, de-seeded and sliced into rings
2 tomatoes, sliced

Heat the contact grill to High. Grease the baking dish.

Melt the butter in a pan on the grill plate and cook the onion for about 2 minutes, stirring occasionally. Stir in the flour then gradually pour on the milk and bring to the boil. Crumble in the cheese. Remove the pan from the grill and beat in the egg yolks. Stir in the breadcrumbs, parsley and sauce and season with salt and pepper.

Stiffly beat the egg whites and fold them into the cheese

mixture. Pour into the baking dish and level the top. Arrange the pepper rings and tomato slices to decorate the top.

Cook between the grill plates for about 15 minutes, until the pudding is set but not dried out. Serve hot.

A light, crisp green salad with an orange or lemon dressing is a lovely accompaniment.

CHEESE ROULADE

A very interesting and enterprising 'cheese roll', made easy on the magic machine.

    6 large eggs, separated
    6 spring onions, finely chopped
    60 ml (4 tablespoons) chopped mixed herbs, eg parsley,
        mint, marjoram
    25 g (1 oz) Cheddar cheese, grated
    salt and freshly ground black pepper

For the filling
    3 hard-boiled eggs, finely chopped
    25 g (1 oz) Cheddar cheese, grated
    50 g (2 oz) cottage cheese
    15 ml (1 tablespoon) double cream
    15 ml (1 tablespoon) chopped chives

Heat the contact grill to High. Grease a Swiss roll tin, line it with greaseproof paper and grease again.

Beat well the egg yolks, then beat in the onions, herbs and 25 g (1 oz) cheese. Season with salt and pepper. Whisk the egg whites until they are stiff, then, with a metal spoon, fold them into the basic mixture. Pour into the tin, level the top and bake between the grill plates for about 5 – 7 minutes, or until the roulade is just set. Leave in the tin to cool.

Mix together the hard-boiled eggs, 25 g (1 oz) grated cheese, cottage cheese, cream and chives.

Turn the roulade on to a piece of greaseproof paper, spread with the filling and roll up, Swiss roll fashion. Serve cold with, perhaps, tomato salad.

This quantity fits a standard Swiss roll tin 23 × 30 cm (9 × 12 in). In a smaller tin (on a small appliance) bake the mixture in 2 batches. Sprinkle a little extra grated cheese over the top layer before cooking. Sandwich them together with the egg filling.

Serves 6

FLAMENCO EGGS

An easy starter or a quick light meal.

> 2 medium-sized tomatoes, skinned and sliced
> 1 canned pimento, drained and chopped
> 100 g (4 oz) button mushrooms, sliced
> 8 stuffed olives, sliced
> salt and freshly ground black pepper
> 40 g (1½ oz butter)
> 4 eggs
> paprika, to garnish

Heat the contact grill to High.

Grease four individual ramekin dishes (first checking that they are the right height to fit between the grill plates; or use small foil cases). Divide the vegetables between the dishes. Season them with salt and pepper and dot with butter.

Arrange the ramekins in the baking dish and partly fill it with hot water. Cook between the grill plates for 5 minutes, stirring the vegetables once. Reduce the heat to Medium.

Break an egg into each dish, sprinkle with a pinch of paprika and cover the baking dish with foil. Cook between the grill plates for about 3 — 4 minutes, until the eggs are just lightly set. Serve hot.

SPANISH OMELETTE

With other vegetables, from the garden, you could make it English omelette, just as easy.

  30 ml (2 tablespoons) vegetable oil
  3 medium-sized onions, sliced
  2 green peppers, de-seeded and thinly sliced
  1 garlic clove, crushed
  3 large tomatoes, skinned and sliced
  10 ml (2 teaspoons) chopped parsley
  8 eggs
  salt and freshly ground black pepper
  25 g (1 oz) butter

Heat the contact grill to High.

Heat the oil in the baking dish and fry the onions and peppers for 2 minutes, stirring frequently. Add the garlic, tomatoes and parsley and fry for 1 minute more.

Beat the eggs in a bowl with salt and pepper and stir in the vegetable mixture.

Make the omelette in one or two 'batches' according to the size of your appliance. Melt the butter, or half of it, in the baking dish and pour in the egg mixture — or half of it. Stir well to distribute the vegetables evenly and cook, between the grill plates, for about 3 minutes, or until the omelette is lightly set.

There are two ways to serve it — hot or cold. Perhaps surprisingly, it's delicious sliced and cold, with salad.

PARSNIP TOASTIES

Do you get the idea? It's a thick purée of root vegetables — and you can make all sorts.

  225 g (8 oz) parsnips, scraped
  225 g (8 oz) potatoes, peeled and scraped

salt
40 g (1½ oz) fine oatmeal
2 spring onions, finely chopped
15 ml (1 tablespoon) chopped chives
freshly ground black pepper
a pinch of grated nutmeg
1 egg, beaten
25 g (1 oz) breadcrumbs (contact grill only)

Cook the parsnips and potatoes together in boiling, salted water until they are tender. Drain and mash them. Stir in the oatmeal, onion and chives and season with pepper and nutmeg. Mix in enough of the beaten egg to make a stiff paste.

Contact grill
Heat the appliance to High. Grease the baking dish.

Mould the vegetable paste into eight small cakes and toss them in the breadcrumbs. Arrange them on the baking dish. Cook between the grill plates for 2 minutes, turn them over and cook for a further 1 – 2 minutes, until the cakes are evenly brown. Serve hot.

Sandwich maker
Heat the appliance. Grease the plates.

Divide the mixture to fill the plates — it must touch both the top and bottom ones — and cook for 2 – 3 minutes, until they are golden brown.

Serve these vegetable cakes as an accompaniment to fish or meat dishes, as a light main dish with other vegetables or a salad, or as a snack topped with tomato or Worcestershire sauce and popped in a pitta (page 196).

6   Sandwiches

Banana and date sandwiches of home-baked wholemeal bread; rare beef and horseradish or salt beef and gherkin on rye; real jam butties, with sliced bread straight from the packet; cinnamon toasties with cottage cheese middles; or bacon and egg doorsteps for breakfast — sweet or savoury — schoolboy specials or party pinwheels; you can make them all to perfection on a sandwich toaster, and to a high degree of satisfaction on a contact grill.

The booklets produced to accompany the appliances are full of so many bright ideas for toasted sandwiches — one lists a hundred possible fillings — that it's a mind-boggling challenge to add to them. Canned meat pie filling or left-over cold meat; kidney beans with coleslaw, and spaghetti with bacon; leeks in cheese sauce, and canned fruit in chocolate sauce — you could, if you owned a computer, produce a different combination of outsides and middles for each and every meal of the year. Some would be delicious; and others would be, well, 'interesting'.

Let's start at the beginning, with the method. Firstly, the term 'toasted' is slightly misleading. Toast — in my book — implies dry bread, unbuttered bread, cooked crisp and brown and still dry under high heat. Sandwiches for toasting, however, are either greased on the outside, or the grill plates are greased. And so the effect is, actually, more like frying in the minimum of fat. If you're like me, and always forget to take butter or hard margarine out of the refrigerator in time to make it spreadable, then it's easier to put a tiny knob on to each grill plate and brush it over with a pastry brush. Or use soft margarine! Flavoured butters (pages 49–51) add enormous variety and individuality, and meat dripping recalls, for me, memories of long ago.

Bread

You can use almost any kind of bread, plain or fancy. Quickest and easiest are the ready-sliced kinds, wholemeal, brown or white. Choose the medium thickness. Even the dullest of everyday breads improve greatly when they're toasted. Day-old loaves are easier to slice than ones still warm from baking — and this is important. If new bread goes into holes the filling seeps through, spoils the appearance and leaves you with a burnt offering to clean from the grill plates.

Fancy breads make fancy sandwiches. Try your own soda bread, herb and cheese bread (pages 177 and 178), light or dark rye, French bread, milk bread, malt bread, fruit bread, caraway bread – as you like it. I have found that rye breads need a little more butter or margarine than usual, or they become too dry; and malt and fruit breads – with currants or sultanas – need a shorter cooking time, or they burn. The only one I haven't been successful with is one of my favourites, stiff-as-a-board black pumpernickel.

Types of sandwich

A sandwich maker produces beautifully neat, sealed little sandwich parcels, puffed up and golden, inviting and delicious. Almost like magic, even the most clumsily-made sandwiches are transformed in moments. On a contact grill, the sandwiches emerge four-square; no fancy shapes and no permanently sealed edges, but with all the goodness and all the flavour.

● Try 'pocket' sandwiches for a change, thick slices of bread cut not quite through, and the filling packed in, pitta style. There's a recipe for pizza pockets, too, on page 194.

● Try toasting teacakes, buns, baps (granary ones are fantastic), oatcakes and rolls of all kinds — with and without fillings. For example, spread split teacakes with crunchy peanut butter or with chopped walnuts and honey, then sandwich them together again before toasting. Pep up left-over cheese and ham rolls from yesterday's packed lunch by popping them in the grill; as always, height is the only limitation. You might have to shave a slice off the top to make them fit. Or slightly hollow out bread rolls and spoon in — what? — sautéed bacon and mushrooms, chopped cooked chicken in parsley sauce, or flaked cooked fish tossed with tarragon and grated cheese.

● Try dipping sandwiches into beaten egg before toasting — it makes the world of difference. Season the egg with salt and pepper for savoury ones, and add crushed garlic, chopped herbs, a few drops of red pepper, soy or Worcester-shire sauce if you like. For sweet ventures, add caster or soft light brown sugar — no more than 10 ml (2 teaspoons) to each beaten egg, or it burns — honey, treacle, grated orange or lemon rind or ground spices. A cinnamon and beaten egg dipping turns everyday sandwiches into the 'Poor Friars' or 'Poor Knights' of French cuisine. One large beaten egg is enough to coat two sandwiches on both sides. Allow one minute extra on the cooking time.

● Try, on a contact grill, toasted open sandwiches. With a standard pizza topping on crumpets (pikelets) or a sturdy slice of bread you have 'instant Italy' (or at least a copy-cat version); with sliced ham and pineapple you have a tasty morsel indeed; and with cream cheese and canned peaches sprinkled with mixed spice and demerara sugar, you have a scrumptious pudding.

● Try garlic bread, again on a contact grill — it's a

marvellous accompaniment to everything from soup to salad. Make vertical slits in a stick of French bread. Spread both sides of the slits generously with garlic butter (page 50), foil-wrap and cook at High heat between the grill plates for 6 – 8 minutes. Or copy the idea with herb and other flavoured butters.

● Try taking toasted sandwiches when you need 'something hot' on winter picnics, on fishing expeditions or on the football terraces. Wrap them closely in a double layer of foil, then in a towel or teacloth and they should still be hand-warming in a couple of hours.

● Try suiting your sandwiches to your schedule. Make them in advance, close-wrap in film or foil and freeze them, or store for one to two days in the refrigerator. When cooking straight from the freezer, allow an extra one to two minutes, according to the filling.

● Try being really mean-minded about all left-overs. Make a basic *thick* white sauce (page 191) and it's a vehicle for chopped cooked meat, poultry or fish. For good measure, you can add a dash of colourful cooked vegetables – a few peas, green beans or diced carrots, for example.

Sweeten the sauce with sugar or honey and add chopped fresh or cooked fruits of all kinds, from the first strawberries of the season to the last apples from the freezer.

● Try getting used to the idea (easy when you cook on a contact grill or sandwich maker) that a pastry turnover, slice or pasty is only a sandwich with different 'outsides'. Mix and match pastry and sandwich fillings throughout the book and your repertoire just grows and grows.

● Really study *your* instructions that come with *your* appliance. If it's a sandwich maker, get to know the exact size to cut the bread, how much filling it will take (to the depth of the gap between the plates) and, if it cuts the sandwiches in halves, how best to distribute the filling. I even know some people who have cut a melamine template and zip round it, whipping off the crusts and cutting the sandwiches to size in one fell swoop. But that's too scientific for me!

'Ordinary' sandwiches

The variations for savoury and sweet sandwiches are endless on both your appliances. Use these suggestions to inspire you to greater heights.

BEEF AND HORSERADISH

> 4 medium-thick slices of bread, wholemeal, brown or
>   white
> butter or margarine, for spreading, or brushing the grill
>   plates
> about 75 — 100 g (3 — 4 oz) cold, cooked beef, sliced
> 30 ml (2 tablespoons) mayonnaise
> 15 ml (1 tablespoon) horseradish relish (or more to taste)
> 2 small pickled gherkins, finely chopped

Spread the bread sparingly on one or both sides with butter or margarine. It is not necessary to butter the inside of the sandwiches, especially when a moist filling is used. It's a matter of choice. Or, melt a very little fat on the grill plates just before cooking, and brush it over evenly.

Contact grill
Heat the grill to High.

Arrange the beef on two slices of bread (if appropriate, buttered side out). Mix together the mayonnaise, relish and gherkins and spread over the meat. Cover with the other two slices.

Toast the sandwiches between the grill plates, in close contact, for about 3 — 4 minutes. If you like, to achieve the criss-cross effect, give them a half-turn at half-time.

Sandwich maker

Heat the appliance.

Cut the bread to fit, trimming off the crusts if you like. If your sandwich maker cuts the sandwiches in halves, make its job easier by cutting the meat slices too. Or cut the meat into thin matchstick strips. Mix the mayonnaise, relish and gherkins. Arrange the meat slices on two slices of bread and spread with the flavouring. Or stir chopped meat into the horseradish mixture and spread on to the bread. Cover with the remaining two slices of bread and grill for 3 — 4 minutes.

Makes 2 sandwiches

For a change

These recipes, following a similar method, all make two sandwiches, generously filled.

Pork and apple

     about 75 — 100 g (3 — 4 oz) cold cooked pork, sliced
     30 ml (2 tablespoons) thick apple purée, or apple sauce
     1 dessert apple, peeled, cored and grated or very finely
          chopped
     a small pinch of mixed spice

Lamb and cucumber

     about 75 — 100 g (3 — 4 oz) cold cooked lamb, sliced
     10 cm (4 in) piece of cucumber, peeled and very finely
          chopped
     15 ml (1 tablespoon) mint jelly

Chicken and pineapple

     100 g (4 oz) cold cooked chicken, chopped
     30 ml (2 tablespoons) pineapple pieces, well drained
     15 ml (1 tablespoon) mango chutney, finely chopped

Mix the ingredients together, spread on two slices of the bread.

Mackerel and lemon
>2 small mackerel fillets, skinned and finely chopped
>grated rind and juice of ½ a lemon
>10 ml (2 teaspoons) chopped chives
>15 ml (1 tablespoon) mayonnaise

Mix the ingredients together and use as a spread. This filling is especially good with wholemeal bread.

Devilled ham
>75 g (3 oz) ham, minced or finely chopped .
>25 g (1 oz) butter or margarine, softened
>10 ml (2 teaspoons) Worcestershire sauce
>2.5 ml (½ teaspoon) Dijon mustard
>freshly ground black pepper
>1 large tomato, thinly sliced

Cream the ingredients together and use as a spread. Top with the tomato slices.

'Liptauer' cheese
>75 g (3 oz) cream cheese
>25 g (1 oz) butter or margarine, softened
>2.5 ml (½ teaspoon) made English mustard
>2 anchovy fillets, chopped
>2 small gherkins, finely chopped
>a large pinch of paprika
>freshly ground black pepper

Beat the cream cheese and butter, then beat in the remaining ingredients. Use as a spread.

Crab and cream cheese
>50 g (2 oz) cream cheese
>25 g (1 oz) butter or margarine, softened
>50 g (2 oz) dressed crab
>salt and freshly ground black pepper

a pinch of cayenne
1 large tomato, sliced

Beat the cream cheese and butter, then beat in the crab and seasoning. Use as a spread.

Cheese and watercress
50 g (2 oz) Cheddar cheese, grated
30 ml (2 tablespoons) chopped watercress
15 ml (1 tablespoon) double or soured cream
freshly ground black pepper

Stir all the ingredients together and use as a spread. Add a sliced tomato for extra colour if you wish.

Egg and bacon
3 rashers streaky bacon, de-rinded
1 hard-boiled egg, chopped
15 ml (1 tablespoon) mayonnaise
2 stuffed olives, chopped
freshly ground black pepper

Grill the bacon rashers between the grill plates (in either contact grill or sandwich maker). Chop the bacon and mix it with the remaining ingredients. Use as a spread.

Herb pâté
75 g (3 oz) soft liver pâté
15 ml (1 tablespoon) chopped parsley or other fresh herb
1 hard-boiled egg, chopped
salt and freshly ground black pepper

Beat the ingredients together and use as a spread. For a change, top with thinly sliced button mushrooms.

Maryland chicken
　　50 g (2 oz) cold cooked chicken, chopped
　　1 banana, mashed
　　15 ml (1 tablespoon) canned sweetcorn, drained

Mix the ingredients together and use as a spread.

Prawns in garlic
　　25 g (1 oz) garlic butter (page 50), softened
　　1 hard-boiled egg, chopped
　　a pinch of cayenne
　　75 g (3 oz) shelled prawns

Beat together the butter and chopped egg and stir in the cayenne and prawns. Use as a spread.

Banana and date
　　1 banana, mashed
　　75 g (3 oz) dates, finely chopped
　　a few drops of lemon juice

Mix together and use as a spread. Raisins make a delicious alternative to dates. Take care — the filling becomes very hot.

Honey and coconut
　　25 g (1 oz) butter or margarine, softened
　　15 ml (1 tablespoon) thick honey
　　50 g (2 oz) desiccated coconut
　　15 ml (1 tablespoon) chopped walnuts

Beat the butter and honey, stir in the coconut and walnuts and use as a spread.

Cottage cheese and orange
　　75 g (3 oz) cottage cheese
　　1 small orange, segmented and chopped

    a few drops of lemon juice
    15 ml (1 tablespoon) sultanas
    30 ml (2 tablespoons) clear honey
    25 g (1 oz) chopped walnuts

Mix the first four ingredients together and use as a spread.
When these sandwiches are toasted, dribble the tops with
honey and sprinkle with nuts.

Cheese and ginger
    75 g (3 oz) cottage cheese
    5 ml (1 teaspoon) ginger syrup
    2 pieces preserved stem ginger, finely chopped
    15 ml (1 tablespoon) chopped walnuts

Mix together and use as a spread.

Whole strawberry jam
    60 ml (4 tablespoons) whole strawberry jam
    a few drops of lemon juice
    30 ml (2 tablespoons) sponge cake crumbs

Mix together and use as a spread. Bite with caution — the
jam becomes very hot.

Lemon curd and blackberries
    30 ml (2 tablespoons) lemon curd
    45 ml (3 tablespoons) blackberries
    10 ml (2 teaspoons) desiccated coconut

Stir together and use as a spread.

Apricot cream
    8 canned apricot halves, drained and thinly sliced
    30 ml (2 tablespoons) soured cream
    a pinch of mixed spice
    10 ml (2 teaspoons) chopped blanched almonds
    40 g (1½ oz) honey butter (page 50)

Stir the first four ingredients together and use as a spread. When the sandwiches are toasted, top them with a pat of honey butter.

SUMMER PUDDING SANDWICHES

These can be made in both appliances.

8 slices of fruit bread, or 16 if they are very small
butter or margarine, for spreading
225 g (8 oz) mixed soft fruits, eg strawberries, red-
   currants, raspberries, hulled
40 g (1½ oz caster) sugar, or to taste
30 ml (2 tablespoons) double cream
ice cream, to serve

Heat the grill to High, or heat the sandwich maker.
   Spread the bread on both sides with fat. Mix together the fruit, sugar and cream and make 4 or 8 sandwiches (see ingredients). Toast them for 2 — 3 minutes, taking care the bread does not burn.
   Serve the sandwiches hot, with ice cream.
Makes 4 or 8 sandwiches

SCRAMBLED EGGS IN TOAST

15 g (½ oz) butter
25 g (1 oz) mushrooms, finely chopped
2 eggs
15 ml (1 tablespoon) milk
salt and freshly ground black pepper
30 ml (2 tablespoons) grated Cheddar cheese
4 medium-thick slices of bread
butter or margarine, for spreading or brushing the grill plates

Heat the contact grill to High, or heat the sandwich maker.

Melt the butter in a small pan and fry the mushrooms gently for about 1 minute. Beat together the eggs and milk and season with salt and pepper. Pour the egg mixture into the pan and cook until the eggs are lightly scrambled.

Spread the bread with butter or margarine, or brush the grill plates. Divide the egg filling between two slices of bread and cover with the other two. Toast, on contact grill or sandwich maker, for 3 — 4 minutes.
Makes 2 sandwiches

For a change
Scrambled eggs are a marvellous basis for all kinds of little extras — especially left-overs. Add a few prawns, a little flaked cooked fish, chopped mushrooms, chopped stuffed olives, walnuts . . . For a lower calorie count, replace the Cheddar with cottage cheese.

KIDNEY AND BACON 'POCKETS'

   2 slices of bread, 3 cm (1¼ in) thick
   15 g (½ oz) butter or margarine, plus extra for spreading
      or brushing
   2 lambs' kidneys, trimmed and chopped
   2 rashers streaky bacon, de-rinded and chopped
   2 medium-sized mushrooms, chopped
   10 ml (2 teaspoons) chopped parsley
   salt and freshly ground black pepper

Heat the contact grill to High, or heat the sandwich maker.

Using a very sharp, pointed knife, cut horizontally through each slice of bread, to within 12 mm (½ in) of the two sides and the further edge. Spread the outside with butter or margarine if you wish, or brush it on the grill plates.

Melt the fat in a small pan and fry the kidneys and bacon for about 3 minutes. Add the mushrooms, stir and cook for 1 minute more. Stir in the parsley and season with salt and pepper.

Hold each 'pocket' in your hand and, with thumb and second finger, gently pinch it in from each side, to open the pocket. Divide the filling between them.

Grill the 'pockets' in the contact grill, between the two plates, in close contact, or in a sandwich maker, for about 3 – 4 minutes, or until they are crispy golden brown.
Makes 2 'pocket' sandwiches

For a change
Follow the method, using any of the other sandwich filling suggestions.

PIN-WHEEL TOASTIES

Here's another way to present sandwiches that really look different, and are specially good for parties. You can use any of your favourite spreads.

8 slices of fresh bread, about 6 mm (¼ in) thick, crusts removed
butter or margarine, for spreading or brushing
100 g (4 oz) cream cheese
15 ml (1 tablespoon) chopped parsley
1 garlic clove, crushed
25 g (1 oz) walnuts, very finely chopped

Heat the contact grill to High, or heat the sandwich maker.

Spread the bread on one side with butter or margarine, or brush the grill plates just before toasting.

Mix together the cheese, parsley, garlic and walnuts. Spread the bread on the unbuttered side. Roll each slice up, Swiss roll style, and cut in half.

Arrange the bread rolls on the lower grill plate of a contact grill and toast them in close contact, for about 2 – 3 minutes, until they are golden brown. Or arrange them carefully in the sandwich maker, cutting them into smaller units to fit, if necessary. Grill for about 2 — 3 minutes. Serve hot.

As an alternative
And it's an idea for party snacks — cut each toasted 'bread roll' into 12 mm (½ in) slices to make very pretty pin-wheel 'bites'.

For a change
Use any soft spreadable mixture — the suggestions for 'ordinary' sandwiches, potted meat and fish pastes, soft pâtés or flavoured butters.
Makes 16 rolls

TOASTED OPEN SANDWICHES

For a change of presentation, here are some thoughts on 'single-crust' sandwiches to make on your contact grill, to start *you* thinking along these lines.

Avocado and cheese
    4 rashers bacon, de-rinded and chopped
    4 slices of bread, about 18 mm (¾ in) thick
    English or French mustard, for spreading
    1 avocado, halved, stoned and peeled
    100 g (4 oz) Cheddar cheese, grated

Heat the grill to High.
    Fry the chopped bacon in a small pan, without any additional fat. Keep it warm. Toast the bread on both sides. Spread one side with mustard, cover with the avocado slices and sprinkle on the grated cheese. Stand the open sandwiches in the baking dish and toast between the grill plates for about 2 minutes, or until the cheese melts. Sprinkle with the bacon and serve hot.
Makes 4 open sandwiches

Drug-store breakfast
    4 slices of bread, about 18 mm (¾ in) thick
    butter or margarine, for spreading
    4 slices cooked ham
    4 small bananas, halved lengthways
    10 ml (2 teaspoons) demerara sugar
    60 ml (4 tablespoons) Cheddar cheese, grated

Heat the contact grill to High.

Toast the bread and spread it on one side with butter or margarine. Arrange a slice of ham on each piece of toast. Cover each one with two halves of banana, sprinkle with the sugar and then with the cheese. Grill for 2 minutes, or until the cheese melts. Serve hot.

Makes 4 slices

Pineapple dreams
    4 slices of bread, about 18 mm (¾ in) thick
    225 g (8 oz) cottage cheese
    4 canned pineapple rings, drained
    1 large apple, peeled, cored and thinly sliced
    15 ml (1 tablespoon) soft light brown sugar
    2.5 ml (½ teaspoon) ground cinnamon

Heat the contact grill to High.

Toast the bread and spread it with the cottage cheese. Arrange a pineapple ring on each piece, with the apple slices round it. Mix the sugar and cinnamon together and sprinkle on the fruit. Place on the baking dish and grill for about 2 − 3 minutes, until the sugar is toffee-brown and crunchy.

Makes 4 open sandwiches

WELSH RAREBIT

Made in minutes on your contact grill.

    4 slices of bread, about 18 mm (¾ in) thick
    100 g (4 oz) Cheddar cheese, grated

25 g (1 oz) butter or margarine
5 ml (1 teaspoon) mustard powder
1 small onion, grated or finely chopped
60 ml (4 tablespoons) brown ale or dry cider
salt and freshly ground black pepper
parsley sprigs, to garnish

Heat the grill to High.

Put the cheese, fat, mustard, onion and brown ale or cider into a small pan, season with salt and pepper and stir over a low heat until the mixture is smooth and creamy.

Toast the bread, spread with the rarebit mixture and arrange the slices on the baking dish. Toast for 2 minutes to set the topping. Garnish with the parsley and serve hot.
Makes 4 slices

TOASTED CHEESE FINGERS

Quick hot snacks made on the contact grill to serve with soup or drinks.

6 slices of bread, 12 mm (½ in) thick, crusts removed
50 g (2 oz) unsalted butter, softened
75 g (3 oz) Samsoe cheese, grated
5 ml (1 teaspoon) made English mustard
freshly ground black pepper

Heat the grill to High.

Thinly spread one side of each piece of bread with butter and arrange them, buttered side down, on the baking dish. Beat together the remaining butter, the cheese, mustard and pepper and spread on the bread.

Cook between the grill plates for 3 − 4 minutes, or until the cheese is crisp and brown. Cut into fingers and serve hot.
Makes 30 fingers

'POOR KNIGHTS' SANDWICHES

Cheese sandwiches dipped in egg before toasting – they're great with grilled mushrooms and tomatoes, bacon, scrambled eggs or cold ham, or with a poached egg on top. They can be made on either appliance.

    8 slices of bread, about 18 mm (¾ in) thick
    100 g (4 oz) Lancashire cheese, sliced
    made English mustard, for spreading
    2 eggs, beaten
    salt and freshly ground black pepper
    butter or margarine, for brushing

Heat the grill to High, or heat the sandwich maker.

Make four cheese sandwiches, spreading the bread with mustard for extra flavour.

Season the beaten egg with salt and pepper, pour it on to a plate and dip in each sandwich, turning to coat both sides.

Brush the grill plates with fat. Toast the sandwiches for 4–5 minutes, or untill they are crunchily crisp. Serve very hot.
Makes 4 sandwiches

PEACH KNIGHTS

This is not so much a sandwich, more a luxury pudding, made on either machine.

    8 slices of bread, about 12 mm (½ in) thick
    25 g (1 oz) honey butter (page 50)
    4 fresh ripe peaches, skinned, stoned and sliced
    10 ml (2 teaspoons) demerara sugar
    2 eggs, beaten
    10 ml (2 teaspoons) soft light brown sugar
    2.5 ml (½ teaspoon) mixed spice
    butter or margarine, for brushing

Heat the contact grill to High, or heat the sandwich maker.

Spread the bread on one side with the honey butter. Arrange the peach slices on four slices of the buttered bread, sprinkle with demerara sugar and top with the remaining bread (buttered side down). Press well together.

Beat together the eggs, brown sugar and mixed spice. Dip in each sandwich, turning it to coat it on both sides.

Brush the grill plates with fat. Toast the sandwiches for 4 – 5 minutes, or until they are crisp and golden. Serve hot.
Makes 4 sandwiches

BAGUETTE SANDWICH

It's a meal in itself, a small French stick loaf full of goodies – they could be any selection you have to hand. They are made on the contact grill.

> 1 small French stick loaf
> ½ recipe 'Liptauer' cheese (page 123)
> ½ recipe herb pâté (page 124)
> ½ recipe devilled ham (page 123)
> ½ recipe cheese and watercress (page 124)
> 1 tomato, thinly sliced, to garnish
> ½ bunch watercress sprigs, to garnish

Heat the contact grill to High.

Cut vertical slits in the loaf 2.5 cm (1 in) apart, without cutting it through. Spread both sides of the cut bread generously with one of the savoury mixtures. Wrap the loaf closely in foil and place it on the lower grill. Heat between the grill plates for 6 – 8 minutes.

Pop a slice of tomato and a few sprigs of watercress into each slit.

To serve, cut lengthways, in long stripey slices.
Serves 4

Garnishes and decorations

Toasted sandwiches of all kinds are lifted on to an entirely different plane if they are presented well. They positively need the contrast of texture and colour that even a sprig of fresh herb, a few pieces of salad or a little fresh fruit can offer. A slightly more substantial garnish turns a sandwich into a complete and utterly delicious course.

SAVOURY GARNISHES

On busy days when every second counts, you can certainly get away with a few lettuce leaves, a sliced tomato and a spring onion at one side of the serving plate. When time's not quite so precious, it's fun to prepare more decorative garnishes. You can make them in advance and store them in a covered container in the refrigerator. Then bring them out, crisp and cool, the most flattering companion to your toasted sandwiches.

Carrots
Scrub or scrape and trim top and bottom. Cut into match-stick strips or thin slices. For an extra-pretty effect stamp flower or star shapes from slices, using a biscuit cutter or scalloped apple corer. The trimmings go into coleslaw salad, or soup. To make curls, peel long, thin strips using a potato peeler. Roll them up, pierce with a cocktail stick and leave in iced water for 1 hour. Remove the sticks.

Cauliflower
Cut into florets of varying sizes.

Celery
Use only the tender stalks. Scrub under cold, running water. To make 'frills', cut into 10 cm (4 in) lengths. With a sharp

knife, make slits about 3 mm (¼ in) apart from one end to about half-way. Soak 2 hours in ice-cold water, then drain.

Cucumber
Cut matchstick strips, or run the prongs of a fork through the skin to stripe it, then cut in thin slices. To make 'cones' cut from the rim to the centre (the radius) in very thin slices, then wrap over the cut edges to form a cone.

Gherkins
To make 'fans', make close cuts from one end almost to the other. Open out the slices to form a fan.

Lemons
To make 'butterflies', cut into thin slices. Cut each slice in half. Then cut almost through the radius of each half-circle. Open out to butterfly shape. To make cones, follow the instructions for cucumber cones.

Mushrooms
Trim the stalks. Cut through the cap and stalk and make thin slices with their characteristic, and very decorative, shape.

Peppers
Trim off the top and bottom, scrape out the seeds and white pith. Cut into matchsticks, or cut across into thin rings.

Radishes
To make 'roses' trim the top and root end. Make four criss-cross cuts in the top. Leave in ice-cold water for 2 hours. For fans, cut in the way described for gherkins. For 'water-lilies', use a small, sharp, pointed knife. Half-way along the length of the radish, push in the knife point through to the centre. Withdraw the knife and put it in again at right angles to the first cut. Continue all round, making V-shape cuts. Pull the two halves apart.

Spring onions
Trim off the roots, green tops and outer layers. Cut the 'frills' as described for celery.

Tomatoes
Make 'water-lilies' as described for radishes. Or simply cut in slices or wedges.

Flavoured butters
(see pages 49-51) Shape into a roll, cut in slices and then in decorative shapes, using tiny biscuit or aspic cutters.

SWEET DECORATIONS

Apples
Core, but do not peel. Slice and toss in lemon juice to preserve the colour.

Cherries
Use in bunches of two or three. Or frost them by dipping bunches in beaten egg white, then in caster sugar. Leave on greaseproof paper in a dry place for 2 hours.

Grapes
Use tiny bunches. Or frost them as above.

Lemons and oranges
Use slices, wedges, butterflies and cones (see above) or water-lilies (see Radishes).

Leaves
The 'sweet' version of a lettuce leaf — visually at least — can be vine leaves, ivy, blackcurrant (they smell heavenly), blackberry, apple – you name it.

Soft fruits

Raspberries, strawberries and blackberries, with a leaf or two – all are highly decorative. Perhaps even more so when they're frosted (see Cherries).

Flowers

When fresh fruit is scarce, a flower or two – even dried ones – can do wonders. Simple white chrysanthemums, marguerites or a few daisies are delicate; a nasturtium flower adds great colour; a couple of dried helichrysum heads could be re-cycled again and again.

Umbrellas

These tiny pretty Japanese paper umbrellas are delightful – re-usable – and cheap.

7 Griddle Cooking, and Waffles

Little round drop scones shiny with honey; crunchy sesame seed biscuits sweetly spiced; golden brown potato cakes to serve with grills; orange pancakes filled with liqueur-flavoured soured cream — if your contact grill has griddle plates, there's an exciting selection of made-in-moments recipes to make the most of them.

The flat griddle plates, evenly heated and perfect heat conductors, cook in just the same way as the traditional heavy griddle iron. That's why many of these recipes have a nostalgic flavour. They are regional favourites of the past cooked by thoroughly modern means!

Open out the contact grill flat, the two plates side by side, and you have a large heated area to cook a whole batch of biscuits, cookies or scones in a very short time.

If the appliance is already heated and you have cooked a meat, fish or vegetable course in the baking dish, it's a matter of moments to griddle potato cakes to go with them — and a perfect match of textures. In the time it takes to dish up the main course, the accompaniment will be golden brown and ready.

Use the griddle plate for making pancakes and you cut out the flipping and tossing action. Pour the batter on to one griddle plate, close the top plate and the pancake is subjected to even heat from both sides at once.

Not all contact grills have the option of griddle plates, and so wherever possible recipes in this chapter have been adapted for cooking by the 'baking' method. Use the baking dish between the closed grill plates and you can cook all the biscuits, cookies and scones to perfection.

When you grease the griddle plate or baking tray use melted margarine or oil.

DROP SCONES

100 g (4 oz) flour
10 ml (2 teaspoons) baking powder
a pinch of salt
1 egg, beaten
150 ml (¼ pint) milk

Heat the contact grill to High.

Sift together the flour, baking powder and salt, stir in the egg and gradually pour on the milk. Beat until the batter is smooth.

Lightly grease the griddle plate and drop on 10 ml (1 dessertspoon) portions of the batter well apart, to allow them to spread.

When the scones start to bubble, flip them over with a spatula and cook on the other side for a further 2 — 3 minutes, until they are evenly brown.

Drop scones are at their best eaten warm and are so quick to make that it's no problem to cook them at the last minute. If you are not going to serve them straight away, wrap them in a tea towel. This allows them to cool slowly, and remain supple.

Serve them with jam, honey or marmalade, or with fruit purée and cream or cottage cheese.

As an alternative
Use wholewheat flour.

For a change
For sweet scones, add 25 g (1 oz) caster sugar and 15 ml (1 tablespoon) golden syrup or honey to the mixture.

For a savoury accompaniment, when they become a snack in their own right, sandwich the scones in pairs with the tuna filling (page 191) or cheese and parsley filling (page 186)
Makes 18

HUNGARIAN PANCAKES

  150 g (5 oz) flour
  a pinch of salt
  2 whole eggs
  2 egg yolks
  300 ml (½ pint) milk
  caster sugar, to serve
  1 lemon, cut in 6 wedges, to serve

For the filling
  225 g (8 oz) curd cheese
  150 ml (¼ pint) soured cream
  75g (3 oz) caster sugar
  10 ml (2 teaspoons) grated lemon rind
  100 g (4 oz) seedless raisins

Begin by making the filling, which can be kept, covered, in the refrigerator. Beat the curd cheese and gradually beat in the soured cream. Stir in the sugar, lemon rind and raisins.
  Heat the contact grill to High.
  Sift together the flour and salt and beat in the eggs and egg yolks. Gradually beat in the milk and continue beating until the batter is smooth. (Or blend the ingredients in a blender until smooth.)

Grease the griddle plate and the inner rim of two 12.5 cm (5 in) flan rings and arrange them on the griddle. Pour just enough pancake batter into each ring to make a thin layer. When the pancake has set, run a knife round each ring and remove it.

If you do not have suitable flan rings, drop the batter on the griddle from a large spoon and very quickly run a plastic spatula round the edge to contain the shape. The batter sets very quickly, and this is less difficult to do than to describe!

Cook the pancakes for about 2 minutes on the first side, flip them over and cook until the second side is golden brown. Transfer the cooked pancakes to a heated plate and keep them warm. Grease the griddle again before cooking each new batch.

Divide the filling between the pancakes, roll them up and arrange them on the dish. Sprinkle them with the sugar and serve with lemon wedges.

As an alternative
And even quicker. Simply serve the pancakes, Shrove Tuesday style, sprinkled with sugar, and with lemon or orange wedges.
Makes 12 pancakes

ORANGE PANCAKES

A lighter batter that uses no milk and is delicious with a simple fruit garnish.

    100 g (4 oz) flour
    a pinch of salt
    1 large egg
    150 ml (¼ pint) unsweetened orange juice
    150 ml (¼ pint) water
    150 ml (¼ pint) soured cream

15 ml (1 tablespoon) orange liqueur (optional)
caster sugar, to serve
1 orange, quartered, to serve

Heat the contact grill to High.

Sift together the flour and salt and beat in the egg. Gradually pour on the orange juice and water, beating all the time and continue doing so until the batter is smooth. (Or put all these ingredients into a blender and blend.)

Cook the pancakes as described in the previous recipe. Spread each one with soured cream, beaten with the liqueur if you use it. Roll them up, arrange them on a heated dish and sprinkle them with sugar. Serve the pancakes with the orange sections.

Makes 8 pancakes

SAVOURY PANCAKES

One of the quickest and simplest light meals to make — and one that must surely have the largest range of variations.

1 recipe standard pancake batter (page 141)

For the filling
25 g (1 oz) margarine
1 medium-sized onion, chopped
175 g (6 oz) bacon, de-rinded and finely chopped
2 cooking apples, peeled, cored and chopped
100 g (4 oz) Cheddar cheese, grated

Heat the contact grill to High.

With the griddle plates in position, melt the margarine in the baking tray and fry the onion and bacon, stirring once or twice, for about 3 minutes. Add the apple and fry for a further 2 minutes. Pour off the fat and mix in half the cheese. Set the filling aside.

Grease the griddle plate and make the pancakes as described on page 142. Divide the filling between the pancakes, roll them up and arrange them in the baking dish. Scatter the remaining cheese over them and grill for 3 minutes.

BORDER PANCAKES

  1 egg
  15 ml (1 tablespoon) sugar
  50 g (2 oz) rolled porridge oats
  50 g (2 oz) flour
  300 ml (½ pint) milk
  maple syrup, treacle or honey, to serve

Heat the contact grill to High.

Beat the egg and sugar together, stir in the oats and flour, then gradually stir in the milk. Beat until the batter is smooth.

Grease the griddle plate. Cook the pancakes as described on page 142. Roll them up, dribble with a little syrup or honey and serve hot.

Makes 8 — 10 pancakes

SOUFFLÉ OMELETTE

Folding the beaten egg whites separately gives a glorious puffy texture that's quite impressive.

  60 ml (4 tablespoons) honey
  6 eggs, separated
  100 g (4 oz) icing sugar, sifted

Heat the contact grill to High.

Put the honey in a small pan and warm it on the griddle plate.

Beat the egg yolks with half the icing sugar. Stiffly whisk the egg whites — fold them into the yolks.

Griddle
Grease a griddle plate and the inner rim of an 18 cm (7 in)
flan ring. Place the ring on the griddle. Pour the egg mixture
into the ring and close the top griddle plate. Cook for about
3 − 4 minutes. Sprinkle with the remaining icing sugar and
grill for 1 minute more, until the sugar caramelizes.

Use two fish slices to lift the omelette on to a heated plate.

Contact grill
Grease the baking tray, pour in the egg mixture and cook as
described for the griddle. Sprinkle on the icing sugar when
the omelette is just lightly set.

Serve the omelette cut in wedges and glazed with the warm
honey.

SPICED FISH CAKES

  225 g (8 oz) cooked white fish, skinned, boned and finely
     flaked
  225 g (8 oz) cooked potato, mashed
  25 g (1 oz) butter
  10 ml (2 teaspoons) Dijon mustard
  2.5 ml (½ teaspoon) curry powder
  salt and freshly ground black pepper
  15 ml (1 tablespoon) chopped parsley
  1 egg, beaten
  50 g (2 oz) breadcrumbs

Mix together all the ingredients except the breadcrumbs,
form the mixture into a ball and chill for 15 minutes. This
makes it easier to shape.

Heat the contact grill to High.

Shape the mixture into flat cakes and toss them in the
breadcrumbs.

Griddle
Grease the griddle plate. Cook the fish cakes for about 3
minutes on each side, until they are golden brown and crisp.

Contact grill
Grease the baking tray. Cook the fish cakes for about 3 — 4
minutes on each side.
    Serve hot.

HAM GRIDDLE SCONES

    225 g (8 oz) plain flour
    15 ml (1 tablespoon) baking powder
    2.5 ml (½ teaspoon) mustard powder
    2.5 ml (½ teaspoon) salt
    freshly ground black pepper
    50 g (2 oz) margarine
    50 g (2 oz) cooked ham, finely chopped
    15 ml (1 tablespoon) chopped parsley or 5 ml (1 teaspoon)
        dried parsley
    about 150 ml (¼ pint) milk

Heat the contact grill to High.
    Sift together the flour, baking powder, mustard, salt and
pepper and rub in the margarine. Stir in the ham and parsley
and mix to a soft but not sticky dough with the milk.
    Roll out on a lightly-floured board to 12 mm (½ in)
thickness. Cut into 7.5 cm (3 in) squares and then triangles.

Griddle
Grease the griddle plate and cook the scones for about 4 — 5
minutes on each side, until they are golden brown.

Contact grill
Grease the baking dish. Cook the scones for about 10 − 12 minutes.

Serve the scones hot, with butter.
Makes about 16 scones

POTATO CAKES

Have the potato 'batter' ready, then cook these crispy, creamy potato cakes at the last minute. They are specially good served with grilled steak or veal.

    5 ml (1 teaspoon) bicarbonate of soda
    700 g (1½ lb) potatoes
    75 g (3 oz) flour
    1 large onion, grated
    2 garlic cloves, crushed
    2 eggs, beaten
    150 ml (¼ pint) single cream
    salt and freshly ground black pepper
    15 ml (1 tablespoon) chopped parsley

Stir the soda into a bowl of water (about 2 litres). Peel the potatoes and coarsely grate them into the water. Leave them to soak for about 1 hour. Drain the potatoes and pat them dry in a clean tea towel.
   Heat the contact grill to High.
   Mix together the flour, onion and garlic, eggs and cream and stir in the potatoes. Season with salt and pepper and stir in the parsley.

Griddle
Well grease the griddle plate. Drop 5 ml (1 teaspoon) portions of the mixture well apart on the griddle and cook for about 2 − 3 minutes on each side until they are golden brown. Grease the plate again before cooking a second batch.

Contact grill
Grease the baking tray. Put little dollops of the mixture (see above) on the tray and cook for about 10 — 12 minutes.

Serve hot.

Makes about 24 potato cakes

POTATO CORNERS

450 g (1 lb) potatoes
salt
15 g (½ oz) margarine
30 ml (2 tablespoons) milk
freshly ground black pepper
100 g (4 oz) canned sweetcorn, drained
100 g (4 oz) rolled porridge oats

Heat the contact grill to High.

Peel or scrape the potatoes and cook them in boiling, salted water until they are tender: 15 — 20 minutes. Mash them with the margarine and milk and season well with salt and pepper. Stir in the sweetcorn and rolled oats and knead to make a smooth dough. Turn the dough on to a lightly-floured board and roll to 6 mm (¼ in) thickness. Cut into triangles.

Griddle
Lightly brush the griddle plate with oil. Cook the triangles for about 3 — 4 minutes on each side, until they are evenly brown.

Contact grill
Grease the baking tray. Cook the triangles for about 6 — 8 minutes.

Serve them hot as a snack, or as a 'vegetable accompaniment' with bacon and eggs or grilled chicken.

POTATO OATIES

    100 g (4 oz) wholewheat flour
    5 ml (1 teaspoon) salt
    100 g (4 oz) rolled porridge oats
    75 g (3 oz) margarine
    100 g (4 oz) cooked potato, mashed or sieved

Heat the contact grill to High.

Mix together the flour, salt and oats, and rub in the margarine. Stir in the mashed potato and knead until the dough is firm and smooth.

Roll out on a lightly-floured board to about 6 mm (¼ in) thickness. Cut into rounds with a 7.5 cm (3 in) biscuit cutter.

Griddle
Cook the biscuits on the griddle for about 3 — 4 minutes on each side, until they are evenly brown.

Contact grill
Cook the biscuits in the baking dish for about 6 — 8 minutes.

Transfer to a wire rack to cool.

Serve the biscuits for breakfast, with honey or marmalade, or with soup and cheese for a snack lunch.

As an alternative
Stir in about 40 g (1½ oz) soft brown sugar after rubbing in the fat, and the biscuits are delicious for tea.
Makes about 16

OAST CAKES

    225 g (8 oz) flour
    5 ml (1 teaspoon) baking powder
    a pinch of salt
    50 g (2 oz) margarine

   25 g (1 oz) demerara sugar
   75 g (3 oz) currants
   10 ml (2 teaspoons) lemon juice
   60 ml (4 tablespoons) water

Heat the contact grill to High.

   Sift together the flour, baking powder and salt and rub in
the margarine. Stir in the sugar and currants and mix to a
soft dough with the lemon juice and water.

   Break the dough into small pieces and roll into circles
about 6 mm (¼ in) thick.

Griddle
Brush the griddle plate liberally with oil or melted butter and
cook the oast cakes for about 3 minutes on each side.

Contact grill
Well grease the baking tray. Cook the cakes for 8 − 10
minutes.

Dust the oast cakes with sugar and eat them hot.
Makes about 18

OAT CAKES

High in fibre and flavour, these crisp biscuits are lovely for
breakfast with honey or marmalade.

   225 g (8 oz) rolled porridge oats
   100 g (4 oz) flour
   2.5 ml (½ teaspoon) salt
   5 ml (1 teaspoon) baking powder
   50 g (2 oz) margarine
   about 60 ml (4 tablespoons) water

Heat the contact grill to High.

   Mix together the oats, flour, salt and baking powder and
rub in the margarine. Mix to a firm dough with the water.
Knead until smooth.

Roll out on a lightly-floured board to 6 mm (¼ in) thick and cut into 7.5 cm (3 in) rounds.

Griddle
Grease the griddle plate and cook the biscuits for about 2 — 3 minutes on each side.

Contact grill
Grease the baking tray. Cook the biscuits for about 6 — 8 minutes.

Cool on a wire rack.
Makes about 16 biscuits

SESAME SEED BISCUITS

100 g (4 oz) margarine
225 g (8 oz) soft light brown sugar
1 egg, lightly beaten
100 g (4 oz) cracked wheat
100 g (4 oz) sultanas
75 g (3 oz) sesame seeds
30 ml (2 tablespoons) milk
225 g (8 oz) wholewheat flour
2.5 ml (½ teaspoon) mixed spice

Heat the contact grill to High.

Beat together the margarine and sugar and gradually beat in the egg. Stir in the wheat, sultanas, sesame seeds and milk. Mix the flour and spice and gradually fold them in. Stir well.

Griddle
Grease the griddle plate, place 5 ml (1 teaspoon) rounds of the mixture well apart, to allow space for spreading. Flatten the rounds with the back of a spoon. Cook for about 3 minutes on each side, until the biscuits are evenly brown.

Contact grill

Grease the baking dish. Make the biscuit rounds as above and cook for about 8 — 10 minutes.

Cool on a wire rack.

Makes about 18 biscuits

COCONUT BISCUITS

100 g (4 oz) margarine
100 g (4 oz) soft light brown sugar
1 egg
225 g (8 oz) flour
5 ml (1 teaspoon) baking powder
grated rind of 1 lemon
75 g (3 oz) desiccated coconut

Heat the contact grill to High.

Beat the margarine and sugar then beat in the egg. Sift together the flour and baking powder and stir into the egg mixture. Stir in the lemon rind and coconut and knead to make a firm dough.

Roll out on a lightly-floured board to a thickness of about 6 mm (¼ in) and cut into 6 cm (2½ in) rounds.

Griddle

Lightly grease the griddle plate and cook the biscuits for about 3 minutes on each side until they are evenly brown.

Contact grill

Grease the baking dish. Cook the biscuits for about 8 — 10 minutes.

Cool on a wire rack.

As an alternative

For almond biscuits, substitute 50 g (2 oz) ground almonds

and 25 g (1 oz) ground rice for the coconut and add a couple of drops of almond essence.
Makes about 16 biscuits

SYRUP BISCUITS

  50 g (2 oz) margarine
  50 g (2 oz) golden syrup
  225 g (8 oz) wholewheat flour
  150 g (5 oz) medium oatmeal
  50 g (2 oz) soft light brown sugar

Heat the contact grill to High.

Put the margarine and syrup in a small pan on the griddle. When it has melted, remove it from the heat, and cool.

Mix together the flour, oatmeal and sugar, pour on the cooled syrup and add just enough milk to give a firm dough.

On a lightly-floured board roll to a thickness of 6 mm (¼ in) and cut into 6 cm (2½ in) rounds.

Griddle
Lightly grease the griddle plate and cook the biscuits for about 3 minutes on each side, until they are evenly brown.

Contact grill
Grease the baking dish. Cook the biscuits for 8 — 10 minutes.

Cool on a wire rack.
Makes about 24 biscuits

HAZELNUT COOKIES

  100 g (4 oz) margarine
  50 g (2 oz) soft light brown sugar
  75 g (3 oz) hazelnuts, chopped
  100 g (4 oz) wholewheat flour
  about 75 ml (3 tablespoons) milk

Heat the contact grill to High.

Cream together the margarine and sugar and stir in 50 g (2 oz) of the chopped nuts. Stir in the flour and just enough milk to make a firm dough. Knead to remove the cracks. Break the dough into walnut-size pieces.

Griddle
Place the dough pieces well apart on the griddle plate, flatten them slightly and sprinkle the remaining nuts on top. Cook for about 3 minutes on each side, until they are evenly brown.

Contact grill
Make the cookies as above but cook them for about 8 − 10 minutes.

Cool on a wire rack.
Makes about 18 cookies

CHOCOLATE BISCUITS

    225 g (8 oz) margarine
    100 g (4 oz) Muscovado sugar
    5 ml (1 teaspoon) vanilla essence
    225 g (8 oz) flour
    50 g (2 oz) powdered chocolate

Heat the contact grill to High.

Cream together the margarine and sugar then stir in the essence. Sift the flour and chocolate powder together, then beat it into the creamed ingredients, a little at a time.

Divide the mixture into pieces, each the size of a large walnut, and roll them into balls.

Griddle
Grease the griddle, place the balls well apart and flatten the tops with a fork. Cook for about 3 minutes on each side.

Contact grill
Grease the baking tray. Prepare as above and then cook for about 8 — 10 minutes.

Cool on a wire rack.
Makes about 24 biscuits

GINGER BISCUITS

225 g (8 oz) flour
100 g (4 oz) margarine
100 g (4 oz) molasses sugar
5 ml (1 teaspoon) ground ginger
100 g (4 oz) cane syrup

Heat the contact grill to High.

Mix all the ingredients together until well blended, then knead until smooth. Roll out on a lightly-floured board until about 6 mm (¼ in) thick and cut into rounds or gingerbread-men shapes.

Griddle
Lightly grease the griddle and cook the biscuits for about 3 minutes on each side, until they are evenly brown.

Contact grill
Grease the baking tray. Cook the biscuits for about 8 — 10 minutes.

Cool on a wire rack.
Makes 8 — 16 biscuits

PEANUT BUTTER COOKIES

75 g (3 oz) margarine
100 g (4 oz) caster sugar
50 g (2 oz) soft light brown sugar

1 egg
100 g (4 oz) peanut butter
175 g (6 oz) flour
5 ml (1 teaspoon) bicarbonate of soda
a pinch of salt
15 ml (1 tablespoon) milk

Heat the contact grill to High.

Cream together the margarine and sugars until the mixture is light and fluffy. Beat in the egg and peanut butter. Sift together the flour, soda and salt and stir into the sugar mixture. Stir in the milk.

Griddle
Lightly grease the griddle plate. Divide the mixture into balls each the size of a walnut, and place well apart. Flatten them with a fork and cook for about 3 minutes on each side.

Contact grill
Grease the baking dish. Make as above then cook the cookies for about 10 — 12 minutes.

Cool on a wire rack.
Makes about 24 cookies

GERMAN HONEY COOKIES

350 g (12 oz) honey
225 g (8 oz) sugar
350 g (12 oz) flour
10 ml (2 teaspoons) ground cinnamon
5 ml (1 teaspoon) ground cloves
5 ml (1 teaspoon) bicarbonate of soda
10 ml (2 teaspoons) water
2 eggs, lightly beaten
100 g (4 oz) chopped mixed candied peel

Heat the contact grill to High.

Put the honey and sugar into a small pan and stand it on a griddle plate to melt. Remove the pan from the heat and cool.

Sift together the flour and spices. Dissolve the soda in the water. Stir the solution into the syrup with the eggs and mixed peel. Gradually pour on to the spiced flour and stir to blend thoroughly. Knead to make a smooth dough.

Roll out the dough into thin sausage shapes about 2.5 cm (1 in) in diameter. Cut off 12 mm (½ in) thick slices.

Griddle
Grease the griddle plate and arrange slices of the dough well apart, to allow space for spreading. Cook the biscuits for about 3 minutes on the first side. Carefully flip them over and cook the second side.

Contact grill
Grease the baking tray. Place the dough slices well apart and cook the cookies for about 8 — 10 minutes.

Transfer the cookies to a wire rack to cool and harden.
Makes about 48 cookies

OATMEAL LACE BISCUITS

    1 egg
    100 g (4 oz) sugar
    10 ml (2 teaspoons) melted butter
    225 g (8 oz) rolled porridge oats
    a pinch of salt
    5 ml (1 teaspoon) vanilla essence

Heat the contact grill to High.

Beat the egg thoroughly, then beat in the sugar. Stir in the melted butter, oats, salt and vanilla.

Griddle
Grease the griddle plate. Drop 5 ml (1 teaspoonful) dollops

of the mixture well apart on the griddle and cook on one side only for about 3 – 4 minutes.

Contact grill
Grease the baking tray. Cook the biscuits for about 5 – 6 minutes with the top grill raised.

Using a fish slice, carefully lift the biscuits on to a cooling rack.
Makes about 16 biscuits

Waffles

Glistening golden with melted butter, fragrant New England maple syrup or pure cane syrup straight from the Caribbean; Balkan-style with soured cream and thick fruit purée; drug-store fashion with cheese or bacon rashers; or wickedly sticky with chocolate sauce. If your appliance has optional waffle plates or you have an electric waffle maker, you can extend delightfully the range of puddings and hot snacks you can prepare and cook in moments.

The basic batter is similar to that for pancakes, though slightly thicker; the fillings and accompaniments can double-up too. See pages 141 and 143 for mouth-watering ideas to adapt. The main difference – apart from the characteristic criss-cross pattern, of course – is that waffles are crisp and almost biscuit-like.

For a change you can substitute up to 45 ml (3 tablespoons) of cocoa powder for one part of flour; add 2.5 ml (½ teaspoon) ground spice; fold in about 45 ml (3 tablespoons) of desiccated coconut or ground nuts; up to 30 ml (2 tablespoons) of sultanas, chopped mixed peel or finely chopped dried apricots, or 50 g (2 oz) of well-drained canned fruit or dessert apples, pears or peaches, all finely chopped.

For a refreshing fruit flavour, substitute part or all of the milk or buttermilk with fruit juice – orange, pineapple or apple juice, the cloudy kind, are all delicious.

For savoury waffles with a difference, fold in 50 g (2 oz) of cottage cheese or grated cheese, finely chopped ham or crisply fried bacon, or 30 ml (2 tablespoons) of chopped herbs.

They really are best eaten at once, straight from the heat. When you are making a large batch, spread them on a rack in a very low oven to keep them warm. Stacking them over hot water, wrapping in a cloth, and other recommended ways of keeping waffles hot do work, but they tend to go soggy.

Waffles freeze perfectly. Cool them on a wire rack, then interleave them with polythene before wrapping and freezing. Remove the plastic layers, spread the waffles on a rack and gently reheat them in a low oven to thaw.

Or cool the waffles, store them in an airtight tin and eat them cold, with butter and honey or jam, or with cheese and an apple or celery.

BASIC WAFFLE BATTER

    100 g (4 oz) flour
    a pinch of salt
    5 ml (1 teaspoon) baking powder
    1 egg
    200 ml (7 fl oz) milk
    25 g (1 oz) butter, melted
    15 ml (1 tablespoon) caster sugar (for sweet waffles)
    margarine or oil, for brushing

To serve
    about 75 g (3 oz) butter, melted or
    about 150 ml (¼ pint) maple syrup or pure cane syrup,
        warmed
    1 lemon, quartered

Heat the contact grill or waffle maker to High.

Sift together the flour, salt and baking powder. Make a well in the centre and beat in the egg, then gradually pour on the milk, still beating. Stir in the melted butter and, for sweet waffles, the sugar.

Brush the waffle plates with margarine or oil. Pour on just enough batter to cover the lower plates, close the top plate and cook for about 3 — 4 minutes, or until the waffles are crisp and dry.

Serve the waffles hot, with melted butter or warmed syrup, and a wedge of lemon. Or with fruit purée, cream or any other weaknesses you may have!

Makes 6 waffles

DAIRY WAFFLES WITH CHOCOLATE SAUCE

    100 g (4 oz) wholemeal flour
    a pinch of salt
    10 ml (2 teaspoons) baking powder
    1 egg
    200 ml (7 fl oz) buttermilk
    25 g (1 oz) butter, melted
    1.5 ml (¼ teaspoon) vanilla essence
    margarine or oil, for brushing

Chocolate sauce
    100 g (4 oz) plain bitter chocolate
    300 ml (½ pint) water
    50 g (2 oz) sugar
    1.5 ml (¼ teaspoon) vanilla essence

Begin by making the sauce. Break up the chocolate and melt it in a bowl over a pan of hot water. Put the water into a small pan, add the sugar and stir until it dissolves. Bring to the boil and simmer for 7 minutes. Add the melted chocolate and vanilla essence; simmer for a further 5 minutes. Serve the sauce hot. (It also keeps will in a covered container in the refrigerator, and can be frozen.)

Heat the appliance to High.

Make the waffle batter as described in previous recipes. Tip in any bran remaining in the sieve. Brush the waffle plates with margarine or oil. Cook the waffles for about 3 − 4 minutes, or until they are crisp and dry. Serve the waffles hot, with the chocolate sauce.

Makes 6 waffles

CHEESE AND BACON WAFFLES

Perfect for breakfast, brunch, lunch and on through to late-night supper.

    100 g (4 oz) flour
    a pinch of salt
    5 ml (1 teaspoon) baking powder
    1 egg
    120 ml (4 fl oz) milk
    120 ml (4 fl oz) natural yoghurt
    50 g (2 oz) Wensleydale or other cheese, grated
    15 ml (1 tablespoon) chopped parsley
    25 g (1 oz) butter, melted
    margarine or oil, for brushing
    8 rashers of bacon, rind removed

Heat the appliance to High.

Make the waffle batter as described previously, folding in the yoghurt, cheese and parsley before stirring in the melted butter. Brush the waffle plates with margarine or oil. Cook the waffles as described, until they are crisp and dry.

Grill the bacon and serve hot, crispy waffles with hot, crispy bacon.

8 Baking

Little pizzas oozing with cheese and anchovies; crispy and light choux buns disappearing in a froth of blueberry cream; Greek-style Baklava, wickedly sticky with honey and nuts; scones and bread rolls with that just-baked smell — are all made in moments on both sandwich maker and contact grill. With the greater versatility offered by the grill, the feast extends to moist and marvellous gingerbread, flapjacks, shortbread and even meringues.

On a sandwich maker, you can cook 'pastry parcels' of all kinds, using shortcrust, rich shortcrust, flaky, puff or even strudel pastry (used as the bread in sandwiches) to enclose sweet or savoury fillings. But it doesn't stop there.

Choux paste puffs up, light as a feather, leaving plenty of space and scope for the imagination when it comes to fillings — sweetened whipped cream, herb-flavoured cream cheese and thick white sauce tossed with shrimps, are just a few.

You can't bake a Victoria sponge sandwich on a sandwich maker, but you can drop the mixture in spoonfuls on to the greased and heated plates and make 'sponge drops' to fill with jam and cream, or to make trifle sponges. Flavour the basic recipe with coconut, caraway, orange or lemon rind and so on and you have a range of fairy cakes for tea-time favourites.

Still with the sandwich maker, you can bake scones – date, nut, raisin, cheese — and even bread rolls. In 25 minutes from taking the flour bin from the shelf — weighing, measuring, mixing, beating and all — I had a batch of wholewheat scones and soda bread rolls cooling on the rack.

If you are in the habit of making your own bread, it's useful to know that lovely light yeasty rolls cook in the sandwich maker in 10 – 12 minutes. And if you're not, you can buy the 'partly-baked' kind. Bread rolls or French sticks (cut in thick slices) cook in only 5 minutes.

Anything you can cook on a sandwich maker and most of the things that you can cook in an oven, you can also cook on a contact grill. The only taboos are the 'high-rise', rather refined bakes for there just isn't space between the grill plates.

Never over-fill a baking dish or sandwich tin with a mixture that's going to rise. If it cooks successfully (and it will) it will hit the top grill plate, flatten out and possibly burn. It is better by far to divide the mixture into two batches for with such short cooking times it's not excessive trouble.

Level the tops of all sponge mixtures, choux pastes, meringues, and then don't go too far away; this isn't a 'cook now, look much later' method. It's fast, and particularly with 'tea-time' baking the timing is critical.

When you try each recipe for the first time, check just *before* the cooking time is up. The recipes have been tested on several different appliances, but each one has its own special characteristics and cooking times do vary slightly. Once you get to know the idiosyncrasies of your own appliance, you will soon know whether, on your machine, 'about 15 minutes' should read exactly 14, 15 or 16 minutes. Once you have checked make a note in the margin. That's the time to follow slavishly in future.

WHOLEWHEAT SHORTBREAD

    350 g (6 oz) wholewheat flour
    100 g (4 oz) soft dark brown sugar
    225 g (8 oz) butter

Heat the contact grill to High.

In a bowl, mix together the flour and sugar and rub in the butter until it is like crumbs, then knead the mixture, still in the bowl, until there are no more cracks.

Grease the baking dish if necessary. Turn the mixture into the dish and press it with your knuckles to fill the corners and smooth the top.

Bake for 12 — 15 minutes. Remove the dish from the heat, score the shortbread into fingers and cool in the dish. Store in an airtight container.

For a change
Chocolate shortbread

Use 100 g (4 oz) wholewheat flour, 50 g (2 oz) ground rice and 30 ml (2 tablespoons) cocoa. Mix these ingredients with the sugar and rub in the butter.

This quantity is for baking in a dish 18.5 × 30 cm (7½ × 12 in). Halve the ingredients or bake in two batches if using a smaller appliance.
Makes 24 fingers

CHEESE SHORTBREAD

It melts in the mouth and is always popular with drinks or coffee.

    100 g (4 oz) flour
    a pinch of cayenne
    a pinch of mustard powder
    50 g (2 oz) semolina
    salt and freshly ground black pepper
    100 g (4 oz) unsalted butter
    100 g (4 oz) Gouda or Edam cheese, grated
    1 small egg, beaten

Heat the contact grill to High.

Sift or mix together the flour, cayenne, mustard, semolina, salt and pepper. Rub in the butter, stir in the cheese and mix well together. Add a little of the egg and mix to a firm dough.

Grease the baking dish if necessary. Press the mixture into it, filling out the corners and levelling the top. Mark the top into finger shapes and brush lightly with the egg.

Close the lid and bake for about 12 minutes. Leave in the dish to cool. Store in an airtight tin.

This amount suits a baking dish 18.5 × 30 cm (7½ × 12 in). Make a proportionately smaller quantity, or bake in two batches, if yours is different.

Makes 24 fingers

HONEY FLAPJACKS

150 g (5 oz) butter
150 g (5 oz) thick honey
225 g (8 oz) muesli, with dried fruit and nuts

Heat the contact grill to High.

Put the butter and honey in a small pan and stand it on a grill plate to melt. Stir in the muesli.

Spread the mixture in the baking dish (greased if necessary) and smooth it out, right into the corners.

Bake for about 15 minutes. Take the tray from the heat and score the flapjack into fingers. Leave in the tray to cool. Store in an airtight container.

As an alternative

Instead of the muesli, use 225 g (8 oz) rolled porridge oats and 75 g (3 oz) currants or sultanas. Also you can exchange the honey with golden syrup, black treacle or molasses, or 150 g (5 oz) demerara sugar.

This quantity is for a baking tray 18.5 × 30 cm (7½ × 12 inches). Halve or bake in two batches if using a smaller appliance.

Makes 24 fingers

VICTORIA SPONGE SANDWICH OR FAIRY CAKES

It's no surprise that you can make two sandwich layers on the contact grill; but it's rather exciting to know you can make a batch of small cakes, some with added flavourings, on the sandwich toaster.

175 g (6 oz) self-raising flour
7.5 ml (1½ teaspoons) baking powder
1.5 ml (¼ teaspoon) salt
175 g (6 oz) caster sugar
175 g (6 oz) soft margarine
3 large eggs
30 ml (2 tablespoons) milk

Have all the ingredients at room temperature. Sift the flour, baking powder and salt together and beat in the remaining ingredients.

Contact grill
Heat the grill to High. Grease two 18.5 cm (7½ in) sandwich tins.

Divide the mixture between the two tins. Bake for about 15 minutes, then allow to cool in the tin before turning out.

You can sandwich the two layers together with jam and/or whipped cream, with butter icing or lemon curd.

Sandwich maker
Heat the appliance. Brush the plates with butter.

Drop spoonfuls of the mixture on to the plates and cook for 4 — 5 minutes. Time very carefully and check the cakes quickly — the mixture is rather inclined to burn. Split the cakes in half and fill with jam or cream, or use them as trifle bases.

For a change
Flavour the mixture with caraway seeds, coconut, grated lemon or orange rind, as you will.
Makes about 16 cakes

COCONUT CAKES

For this recipe you can use your sandwich maker as well as the contact grill.

    225 g (8 oz) flour
    a pinch of salt
    10 ml (2 teaspoons) baking powder
    100 g (4 oz) butter
    175 g (6 oz) sugar
    2 large eggs, lightly beaten
    75 g (3 oz) desiccated coconut

Sift together the flour, salt and baking powder. Cream the butter and sugar and gradually beat in flour and eggs alternately. Stir in the coconut.

Contact grill
Heat the contact grill to High. Spoon the mixture into eighteen paper baking cases. Arrange them in the baking dish and bake for about 15 minutes.

Sandwich maker
Heat the appliance. Brush the plates with melted butter.
    Drop heaped tablespoons of the mixture on to the sandwich plates and cook for about 5 minutes.

For a change
Instead of the coconut, you can flavour this versatile basic mixture with 15 – 30 ml (1 – 2 tablespoons) caraway seeds, or with 50 g (2 oz) chopped crystallized cherries.

Makes about 18 cakes

SPICED PEEL CAKES

You can use both appliances for these cakes.

    225 g (8 oz) self-raising flour
    5 ml (1 teaspoon) mixed spice
    2.5 ml (½ teaspoon) ground ginger
     a pinch of ground cloves
    a pinch of salt
    75 g (3 oz) hard margarine
    50 g (2 oz) demerara sugar
    50 g (2 oz) chopped mixed candied peel
    about 45 ml (3 tablespoons) milk, to mix

Sift together the flour, all the spices and salt and rub in the margarine until the mixture is like crumbs. Stir in the sugar and peel and mix to a stiff dough with the milk.

Contact grill
Heat the grill to High. Grease the baking dish if necessary.
    Using 2 spoons, put heaps of the dough on the dish – each one about 10 ml (2 teaspoons). Bake for about 15 minutes. Cool on a rack.

Sandwich maker
Heat the appliance. Brush the plates with butter.
    Drop tablespoons of the mixture on to the plates and cook for about 8 minutes.

For a change
Use currants, sultanas, raisins, chopped dried dates or —
delicious — apricots in place of the candied peel.
Makes about 18

GINGER AND LEMON SQUARES

100 g (4 oz) margarine
200 g (7 oz) soft dark brown sugar
3 eggs, lightly beaten
225 g (8 oz) self-raising flour
2.5 ml (½ teaspoon) salt
5 ml (1 teaspoon) ground ginger
3 pieces preserved ginger, drained and finely chopped

For the frosting
50 g (2 oz) margarine
225 g (8 oz) sifted icing sugar
grated rind and juice of 1 lemon

Heat the grill to High. Grease a Swiss roll tin 23 × 30 cm (9 ×
12 in) (or use two smaller tins).

Cream together the margarine and sugar until it is almost
frothy, then beat in the eggs a little at a time. Sift the flour,
salt and ginger gradually into the egg mixture and stir in the
chopped ginger.

Spread the sponge mixture into the tin and bake for 15
minutes, or until the cake is just firm. Leave in the tin to cool.

To make the frosting, melt the margarine in a pan, remove
it from the heat and stir in the icing sugar, lemon rind and
lemon juice. Spread the frosting on the cake and cut into
squares.
Makes about 16 slices

CHOCOLATE FUDGE COOKIES

225 g (8 oz) margarine
225 g (8 oz) soft light brown sugar
225 g (8 oz) self-raising flour
150 g (5 oz) rolled porridge oats
50 g (2 oz) cocoa

For the frosting
50 g (2 oz) margarine
50 g (2 oz) bitter chocolate
225 g (8 oz) sifted icing sugar

Heat the grill to High. Grease the baking dish if necessary.

Put the margarine and sugar into a pan and stand it on one of the grill plates until the fat melts. Stir in the flour, oats and cocoa and mix well.

Turn into the baking dish and level the mixture with the back of a spoon. Bake for 12 — 15 minutes, until the biscuits are crisp. Leave in the tin to cool.

To make the frosting, melt the margarine and chocolate in a pan and beat in the icing sugar. Spread on the biscuits, cut into fingers and carefully remove from the tin.
Makes 18 biscuits

WALNUT ROULADE

3 large eggs, separated
10 ml (2 teaspoons) water
75 g (3 oz) caster sugar
30 ml (2 tablespoons) clear honey
100 g (4 oz) self-raising flour, sifted
75 g (3 oz) ground walnuts
8 walnut halves, to decorate

For the filling
    300 ml (½ pint) double cream, whipped
    30 ml (2 tablespoons) clear honey

Heat the grill to High. Line a Swiss roll tin with greaseproof paper, greased with oil or margarine and dusted with flour, or with vegetable parchment paper.

Whisk the egg whites with the water until they are very stiff. Gradually add the sugar, beating all the time. When the mixture is stiff again, add the egg yolks and honey. Stir in the flour and nuts. Turn the mixture into the tin and bake for about 12 minutes. The sponge should be firm to the touch.

Tip the roulade on to a sheet of sugar-dusted greaseproof paper and roll up, complete with the lining paper. Leave to cool.

Stir the honey into the cream. When the roulade is cool, unroll it, peel off the paper and spread with cream. Roll it up again and sprinkle with caster sugar. Decorate with walnut halves.

A small contact grill will not take a Swiss roll tin. Bake the mixture in two batches and sandwich them together with half the cream. Spread the other half on top and decorate with walnuts. It makes a different shape, but still has the same flavour!

Makes 1 roulade

TREACLE GINGERBREAD

Moist, dark and sticky, this cake doesn't really develop its full flavour until it has been stored for four to five days.

    100 g (4 oz) butter
    30 ml (2 tablespoons) golden syrup
    30 ml (2 tablespoons) black treacle
    100 g (4 oz) plain white flour

    2.5 ml (½ teaspoon) salt
    15 ml (1 tablespoon) ground ginger
    2.5 ml (½ teaspoon) ground cinnamon
    5 ml (1 teaspoon) bicarbonate of soda
    100 g (4 oz) wholewheat flour
    40 g (1½ oz) soft dark brown sugar
    50 g (2 oz) sultanas
    150 ml (¼ pint) milk
    1 large egg

Heat the grill to Medium. Line the baking dish with greased greaseproof paper.

Melt the butter, syrup and treacle in a small pan standing on one of the grill plates. Sift together the white flour, salt, spices and soda and stir in the wholewheat flour, sugar and sultanas.

Beat the milk and egg together. Gradually stir into the dry ingredients first the treacle mixture, then the egg and milk. Pour into the prepared dish and bake for about 45 minutes, or until the cake is just firm.

Cool the cake in the tin, then turn it out and wrap it closely in foil to store.

It doesn't really need any additions, but it is absolutely delicious spread with cream or cottage cheese.

This mixture suits a dish 18.5 × 30 cm (7½ × 12 in). Halve the quantity or bake it in two batches if yours is significantly smaller.
Makes about 12 pieces

ALMOND MERINGUES

    2 egg whites
    100 g (4 oz) caster sugar
    50 g (2 oz) ground almonds

15 ml (1 tablespoon) toasted almonds, chopped
15 ml (1 tablespoon) clear honey
150 ml (¼ pint) double cream, whipped

Heat the contact grill to Medium.

Whisk the egg whites until they are very stiff and will stay in peaks. Whisk in half the sugar and beat until the peaks form again. Mix together the remaining sugar and ground almonds and fold into the meringue mixture. Use a metal spoon and a light touch.

Line the baking dish with vegetable parchment (non-stick) paper. Using two tablespoons, divide the mixture into eight even-sized rounds. Bake for 5 minutes. Reduce the heat to Low and bake for a further 15 — 20 minutes, until the meringues are crisp outside. Remove them from the heat and let them cool before you ease them from the baking paper.

Stir the toasted almonds and honey into the cream. Sandwich the meringues together in pairs just before serving.

Meringues cooked on a contact grill will not be 'the same' as those baked in the oven. But just you see how good they are!

For a change
Use 50 g (2 oz) desiccated coconut instead of the ground almonds in the meringue mixture. And for the filling, flavour the cream with the honey, sandwich the meringue halves together, then sprinkle toasted coconut along the line of the cream.
Makes 4 'double' meringues

DATE SCONES

For 'date' you could read sultana, currant, raisin or mixed peel — all dried fruits give good results. They are just as good whether you use your contact grill or your sandwich maker.

225 g (8 oz) wholewheat self-raising flour
15 ml (1 tablespoon) baking powder
2.5 ml (½ teaspoon) salt
40 g (1½ oz) white vegetable fat or margarine
40 g (1½ oz) demerara sugar
75 g (3 oz) chopped dried dates
125 ml (4 fl oz) yoghurt or milk

Sift together the flour, baking powder and salt and tip in any bran from the sieve. Rub in the fat and stir in the sugar and dates. Mix to a stiff dough with the yoghurt or milk. Knead it until there are no more cracks.

Contact grill
Heat the grill to High.

Roll out the dough to 2.5 cm (1 in) thick and cut into rounds, using a 7.5 cm (3 in) cutter. Brush the tops with milk and sprinkle with a little demerara sugar.

Arrange the scones in the baking dish and bake for about 10 minutes, until they are firm. Wholewheat scones do not rise very impressively, but they have a delicious 'nutty' flavour.

Or cook them the lazy way, saving time and washing up: break off pieces of the dough and gently roll them between your palm into sausage shapes. Arrange them on the baking tray.

Sandwich maker
Heat the appliance. Brush the plates with butter.

Drop tablespoons of the mixture on to the plate and cook for about 10 minutes, or until the scones sound hollow when you tap them.

For a change
Substitute 50 g (2 oz) chopped walnuts for the dates. These scones will be less moist so serve them buttered or spread with creamy cheese and honey.
Makes about 12 scones

CHEESE SCONES

Tiny versions are good served hot, with drinks. And they make a change from bread to serve with soup. You can cook them on either appliance.

225 g (8 oz) self-raising flour
10 ml (2 teaspoons) baking powder
2.5 ml (½ teaspoon) salt
2.5 ml (½ teaspoon) cayenne
2.5 ml (½ teaspoon) mustard
40 g (1½ oz) white vegetable fat or margarine
75 g (3 oz) Cheddar cheese, grated
125 ml (4 fl oz) milk

Sift together the flour, baking powder, salt, cayenne and mustard and rub in the fat. Stir in the cheese and mix to a firm dough with the milk. Knead the dough until it is smooth.

Contact grill
Heat the grill to High.
    Roll out the dough to about 2 cm (¾ in) thick and cut into 5 cm (2 in) rounds. Brush the tops with milk.
    Arrange on the baking dish and bake for about 10 minutes, until well risen and a lovely golden brown.

Sandwich maker

Heat the appliance. Brush the plates with butter.

Drop tablespoonfuls of the mixture on to the plates and cook for about 10 minutes, until the scones are firm and golden brown.

For a change

Turn savoury scones into spiced ones. Leave out the cheese. Sift 5 ml (1 teaspoon) mixed spice with the dry ingredients. Measure off 15 ml (1 tablespoon) of the milk and replace it with honey. Gently warm the two together then cool before mixing.

Makes about 12 scones

CHEESE SCONE RING

50 g (2 oz) unsalted butter
225 g (8 oz) self-raising flour
a pinch of salt
about 150 ml (¼ pint) milk
100 g (4 oz) Wensleydale cheese, grated
2.5 ml (½ teaspoon) mixed dried herbs

Heat the grill to High.

Rub the butter into the flour, stir in the salt and mix to a firm dough with the milk. Knead the dough free of cracks, then roll it to measure 23 × 30 cm (9 × 12 in). Sprinkle the cheese and herbs over the dough and roll up like a Swiss roll. Cut it into eight pieces.

Arrange the slices in a circle or oval, just touching each other, in the baking dish. Bake for 10 − 12 minutes, until they are pale golden brown. Leave them in the dish to cool.

These savoury scones are delicious as the centrepiece of a salad meal, served with a dressing of yoghurt, chopped mint and gherkins.

Makes 8 scones

WHOLEWHEAT SODA BREAD

There is no waiting for the dough to rise with this bread. This recipe gives instructions for two loaves cooked in the contact grill, and bread rolls in the sandwich maker.

> 450 g (1 lb) wholewheat flour
> 10 ml (2 teaspoons) bicarbonate of soda
> 10 ml (2 teaspoons) salt
> 300 ml (½ pint) buttermilk or soured milk (see below)
> about 30 ml (2 tablespoons) warm water

Put the flour into a bowl and stir the soda and salt through it. Or sift the three dry ingredients, then stir in the bran that's left in the sieve. Pour on the milk and mix to a firm dough, adding the water if it's needed, to make the dough pliable.

To turn fresh milk sour, stir in 10 ml (2 teaspoons) lemon juice, or use part yoghurt, part milk.

Contact grill
Heat the grill to High.

Divide the dough into two equal pieces. Shape into rounds of about 12 cm (5 in) diameter and place one or both in the dish. Flatten below the level of the tin and mark a cross deep into the top. Cover the dish with foil and bake for 10 minutes. Remove the foil and continue baking for 5 minutes.

The bread is delicious eaten warm from the grill. It's not so good the next day, but it does freeze well.
Makes 2 small flat loaves

Sandwich maker
Heat the appliance. Brush the plates with butter.

Tear pieces off the dough almost the size of small apples. Cook for about 8 minutes, until they are crusty and sound hollow.
Makes about 12 rolls

CHEESE AND HERB SODA BREAD

A recipe for both appliances.

>   450 g (1 lb) wholewheat flour
>   7.5 ml (1½ teaspoons) bicarbonate of soda
>   5 ml (1 teaspoon) salt
>   25 g (1 oz) butter
>   2.5 ml (½ teaspoon) celery seed
>   5 ml (1 teaspoon) dried mixed herbs
>   100 g (4 oz) Cheddar cheese, grated
>   300 ml (½ pint) soured milk

Thoroughly mix together the flour, soda and salt, or sift them and stir in the sieved-out bran. Rub in the butter to distribute it evenly. Stir in the celery seed, herbs and 75 g (3 oz) of the cheese and pour on the milk. Mix to a firm dough and knead until it is smooth and without cracks.

Contact grill
Heat the grill to High.

Divide the dough into two equal pieces. Shape each one into a 15 cm (6 in) round, flatten them and brush the tops with a little milk. Mark each one into four segments and sprinkle on the remaining cheese. Place in the baking dish and bake — one at a time in a small appliance, side by side in a large one. They should be firm and well browned in about 15 minutes.
Makes 2 small, flat loaves

Sandwich maker
Heat the appliance. Brush the plates with butter.

For this method, stir all the cheese into the flour mixture. Tear off pieces of the dough, about the size of small apples, and cook for about 8 minutes, until the rolls sound hollow when you tap them.
Makes about 12 rolls

IRISH SODA BREAD ROLLS

They are delicious whether you use the contact grill or the sandwich maker.

   450 g (1 lb) flour
   5 ml (1 teaspoon) salt
   5 ml (1 teaspoon) bicarbonate of soda
   10 ml (2 teaspoons) cream of tartar
   25 g (1 oz) butter
   300 ml (½ pint) milk

Sift together the flour, salt, soda and cream of tartar and rub in the butter. Mix to a soft dough with the milk. Knead the dough to rid it of cracks.

Contact grill
Heat the grill to High.
   Break the dough into twelve pieces, arrange them on the baking tray and cook them in two or three batches for about 15 minutes. The rolls should feel light and sound hollow. Serve, preferably warm, the same day. Or freeze them.

Sandwich maker
Heat the appliance. Brush the plates with butter.
   Divide the dough into twelve pieces and cook for about 8 minutes, until the rolls are crusty and sound hollow.

For a change
When cooking rolls on the contact grill, you can sprinkle caraway, cumin, fennel, poppy or sesame seeds on top.
Makes 12 rolls

BLUE CHEESE QUICHE

   225 g (8 oz) shortcrust pastry
   175 g (6 oz) cream cheese

75 g (3 oz) blue cheese, crumbled (Roquefort is especially
  tasty)
2 large eggs, lightly beaten
150 ml (¼ pint) single cream
salt and freshly ground black pepper
30 ml (2 tablespoons) chopped chives

Heat the contact grill to High. Grease the baking dish if
necessary, or an 18 cm (7 in) flan ring and a baking sheet.

Roll out the pastry, line the dish or ring with it, trim and
neaten the edges. Prick all over the base with a fork. Line the
pastry with a piece of foil and sprinkle in a layer of dried
beans (about 6 tablespoons of any kind of bean). Bake the
pastry 'blind' in this way for 10 minutes. Remove the foil and
'baking beans'. The beans can be cooled, stored in a
lidded jar and used over again. Lower the heat to Medium.

Beat together the cream and blue cheeses, beat in the eggs
and stir in the cream. Season the custard mixture with salt
and pepper and stir in the chives. Pour into the pastry case.

Bake the flan for 15 — 20 minutes, covering the top with
foil if it becomes too brown.

Serve warm or cold.

To reheat the flan — for it really is much nicer warm —
return it to the grill, set at Medium, for about 10 minutes.

For a change
Instead of the chives, stir in a bunch of watercress chopped
(though reserve a few sprigs to garnish). It's a lovely combination with the blue cheese.
Serves 4 — 6

OATY RATATOUILLE FLAN

75 g (3 oz) 81% wheatmeal self-raising flour
150 g (5 oz) coarse oatmeal

a pinch of salt
100 g (4 oz) margarine
about 60 ml (4 tablespoons) water

For the filling
30 ml (2 tablespoons) vegetable oil
1 large onion, sliced
2 cloves garlic, crushed
1 red pepper, trimmed and sliced, or 1 canned pimento,
     drained and sliced
450 g (1 lb) courgettes, sliced
100 g (4 oz) mushrooms, sliced
450 g (1 lb) tomatoes, skinned and sliced
30 ml (2 tablespoons) chopped parsley
salt and freshly ground black pepper
50 g (2 oz) Gruyère or other cheese, grated

Heat the contact grill to High.

Begin by making the filling. Heat the oil in the baking dish, cook the onion, between the grill plates, for 1 minute, add the garlic and cook for ½ minute, add the pepper and courgettes and cook for 1 minute, then the mushrooms, tomatoes, parsley and seasoning. Stir well and cook for about 10 minutes, until the vegetables are tender but not mushy. Remove from the heat and cool.

While the vegetables are cooking, make the pastry. Mix the flour, oatmeal and salt and rub in the fat. Mix to a firm dough with the water. Roll out and line a greased flan ring and baking sheet, or a baking dish. Prick the base heavily with a fork. Line the case with foil and about 6 tablespoons of dried beans.

Bake the pastry 'blind' like this for 12 minutes. Remove the foil and beans (see page 180) and return the pastry to dry out — another 3 minutes or so.

Pour in the cooled vegetables — they must be cold — and sprinkle on the cheese. Cook between the grill plates for about 5 minutes, until the cheese bubbles. Serve hot or cold.

For a change
This vegetable medley makes a super 'sandwich filling' for pocket pizzas, or can be used as a baked pizza topping, teamed perhaps with salami or ham.
Serves 4 — 6

WHOLEWHEAT FISH AND LEEK FLAN

This crunchy 'brown' pastry, full of fibre and flavour, cooks particularly well on a contact grill.

> 225 g (8 oz) wholewheat flour
> a pinch of salt
> 125 g (5 oz) margarine, or white vegetable fat and margarine mixed
> about 45 ml (3 tablespoons) water

For the filling
> 25 g (1 oz) butter
> 4 medium-sized leeks, thinly sliced
> 15 ml (1 tablespoon) chopped parsley
> 100 g (4 oz) cooked smoked haddock, skinned and flaked
> 300 ml (½ pint) single cream, or milk
> 2 large eggs
> salt and freshly ground black pepper
> 50 g (2 oz) Cheddar cheese, grated
> watercress or parsley sprigs, to garnish

Begin by making the pastry. It needs a half-hour's 'rest'. Stir the flour and salt and rub in the fat. Mix to a firm dough with the water. Wrap in clingfilm or foil and chill for 30 minutes.

Heat the grill to High.

Melt the butter in the baking dish and cook the leeks for 3 minutes between the grill plates. Stir in the parsley and remove from the heat.

Roll out the pastry and line a greased flan ring on a baking sheet, or the baking dish. If the paste is too crumbly to handle, put it on the base and press it out to fill the shape. Knuckles and the back of a tablespoon are ideal for this. Prick the pastry with a fork, line it with foil and dried beans (about 6 tablespoons) and bake for about 12 minutes. Lower the heat to Medium. Tip out the foil and beans (see page 180) and spread the flaked fish and the leeks in the base. Beat together the cream or milk and the eggs and season with salt and pepper. Pour the custard mixture into the flan case, sprinkle on the cheese and bake for about 15 – 20 minutes, until the custard filling is just firm. Decorate with the watercress or parsley. Serve warm or cold.

For a change
If you like this pastry — and it's one of my favourites — use it for all your favourite flan recipes. It's good with the blue cheese mixture (pages 179 – 80).
Serves 4 – 6

CHEESE AND VEGETABLE PASTIES

An excellent recipe for both appliances.

350 g (12 oz) shortcrust pastry
225 g (8 oz) carrots, cooked and diced
175 g (6 oz) canned sweetcorn, drained
15 ml (1 tablespoon) chopped parsley
225 g (8 oz) Cheddar cheese, grated
salt and freshly ground black pepper
milk, for brushing

Roll out the pastry and cut it into eight circles, using a 12.5 cm (5 in) cutter. Or cut shapes to fit your sandwich maker.

Mix together the carrots, sweetcorn, parsley and cheese and season with salt and pepper. Divide the filling between the pastry shapes, spooning it into the centre. Brush the pastry edges with milk. Fold them over and pinch the edges together.

Contact grill
Heat the grill to High. Arrange the pasties on the baking dish (greased if necessary) and brush the tops with milk. Bake for about 15 minutes, until the pastry is crisp and brown.

Sandwich maker
Heat the appliance. Brush the plates with butter. Cook the pasties for about 8 minutes, until they are crisp and golden brown.

Serve hot or cold.

For a change
Here's a fine way to use small amounts of left-over cooked vegetables — peas, cauliflower, French, runner or broad beans, diced parsnips, Jerusalem artichokes, chopped asparagus. Play the matching game for super snacks or picnics, always mixing the vegetables with cheese.
Makes 8 pasties

ALMOND AND HONEY TARTS

Serve at tea-time or as a dessert, warm or cold, with cream, soured cream or yoghurt.

    225 g (8 oz) shortcrust pastry
    45 ml (3 tablespoons) thick honey
    75 g (3 oz) self-raising flour

2.5 ml (½ teaspoon) baking powder
50 g (2 oz) soft margarine
50 g (2 oz) soft light brown sugar
2.5 ml (½ teaspoon) almond essence
100 g (4 oz) marzipan, chopped
1 large egg, lightly beaten
sifted icing sugar, to decorate

Heat the grill to High.

Roll out the pastry thinly and cut into rounds, using a 7 cm (2½ in) cutter. Grease 24 bun tins with oil or melted margarine and line them with pastry circles. Using two spoons to make the job less sticky, put about 2.5 ml (½ teaspoon) of honey into each pastry case.

Sift together the flour and baking powder and beat in the other ingredients, excluding the icing sugar. Beat the mixture until it is well blended. Divide it between the pastry cases.

Bake each tray of tarts for 15 minutes, when the fillings will be rounded and golden brown. Leave to cool a little, then dust the tops with a sprinkling of icing sugar.

As an alternative
If you do not have any ready-made marzipan, substitute 50 g (2 oz) blanched almonds, toasted and chopped, and press a whole almond into the top of each filled tart before baking.

A small appliance won't take a 12-hole bun tin. Use foil tart cases and arrange them in the baking dish, and bake in several batches.
Makes 24

CHEESE AND HERB PIES

Equally good served warm or cold, with a green vegetable or salads, or as a picnic snack, made in either appliance.

225 g (8 oz) puff pastry
milk, for brushing
175 g (6 oz) cottage cheese
50 g (2 oz) Wensleydale cheese, grated
30 ml (2 tablespoons) chopped parsley (broad-leafed, if available)
freshly ground black pepper
a pinch of nutmeg
1 large egg, beaten

Roll out the pastry very thinly and cut eight rectangles of even size — to fit your sandwich maker. Brush the edges of four pieces with milk.

Mix together the cheeses, parsley, pepper and nutmeg and beat in the egg. Divide the filling between the pastry pieces spooning it into the centre. Press on the pastry lids and seal the edges together to close the parcels.

Contact grill
Heat the grill to High. Arrange the four pies in the baking tray and brush the tops with milk. Bake for about 15 minutes, until the pies are puffed up and golden brown.

Sandwich maker
Heat the sandwich maker. Brush the plates with melted butter and cook the pies for about 8 minutes, until they are golden brown.

As an alternative
Use shortcrust pastry instead — you won't get the layered look, but the pies will be just as delicious.

For a change
Turn them into sweet pies, using 175 g (6 oz) cottage cheese, 50 g (2 oz) chopped dried dates, one mashed banana and the

egg. When they are cooked sprinkle with soft light brown sugar and serve with soured cream.

Makes 4

BAKLAVA (HONEY AND WALNUT SLICES)

This makes an impressive party sweet that is definitely proud of its Greek origins. The recipe is suitable for the sandwich maker as well as the contact grill.

> 275 g (10 oz) strudel or filo pastry (see below)
> 175 g (6 oz) chopped walnuts
> 5 ml (1 teaspoon) powdered cinnamon
> 100 g (4 oz) unsalted butter, melted

For the syrup

> 100 g (4 oz) sugar
> 100 g (4 oz) honey
> 425 ml (¾ pint) water
> 15 ml (1 tablespoon) lemon juice

Stir the walnuts and cinnamon together. That's the filling made! Boil the syrup ingredients for 10 minutes, until they become sticky.

You can buy strudel or filo pastry, rolled and packed in boxes, in delicatessen or specialist food shops. The 'leaves' of pastry are almost as thin as tissue paper — and very time-consuming to make at home. If you can't find it, use puff pastry instead. Roll it out thinly and leave out the butter-brushing steps. In this case, follow the straightforward 'sandwich-maker' method for the contact grill, too.

Contact grill

Heat the grill to High. Brush the baking dish with melted butter.

Measure the dish and cut the pastry sheets right through

the whole thickness, to fit — it makes the whole operation much quicker. Line the dish with one pastry sheet, brush it lightly with butter, add another pastry layer and brush with butter. Sprinkle on some nuts, make two more pastry and butter layers, then continue like this, finishing with a double pastry layer. Brush the top with water and mark into eight pieces. Bake for about 10 minutes.

Remove from the heat and allow to cool. Pour over the boiling syrup and again leave to cool. The pastry will absorb the syrup, yet stay crisp.

Sandwich maker
Heat the appliance.

The layer-upon-layer system doesn't work so well by this cooking method. Cut the pastry, right through all the layers to fit your appliance. For each *baklava* slice build up about six layers of pastry, brushing butter between each one. Sprinkle on about 2 cm (¾ in) thickness of the nut mixture, then top it with about six more layers of buttered pastry. Brush the sandwich plates with melted butter. Cook the pastries for about 8 minutes. Don't go too far away – they burn easily.

Transfer the pastries to a baking dish to cool. Pour on the boiling syrup and leave to cool again. They will be crisp, sticky and delicious.
Makes 8 pieces

SEMOLINA CUSTARD PIE

This is the Galactobouriko of Greece, crispy outside, creamy inside, and utterly irresistible.

    350 g (12 oz) strudel or filo pastry (see previous recipe)
    850 ml (1½ pints) milk
    3 medium-sized eggs, separated
    175 g (6 oz) caster sugar

75 g (3 oz) semolina
50 g (2 oz) butter, melted
25 g (1 oz) icing sugar
2.5 ml (½ teaspoon) ground cinnamon

Heat the grill to High.

Heat the milk just to simmering point. Beat the egg yolks in a bowl and beat in the sugar and semolina. Gradually pour on the hot milk, stirring as you do so. Pour the mixture back into the rinsed-out saucepan and stir over very low heat for about 3 minutes, until it thickens. Remove from the heat, stir in the butter and leave to cool. Whisk the egg whites until they are stiff. Fold them into the cooled custard.

Brush the baking dish with butter. Cut the pastry sheets, through all the layers, to fit it (see pages 187−8). Spread half of the pastry sheets to line the pan, brushing each one with butter. Pour on the filling and spread it out evenly. Cover the custard with the rest of the pastry, again brushing each layer with butter.

Mark the top into eight slices and brush with water. Cover the dish with foil and bake for about 10 minutes. Remove the foil and cook for another couple of minutes, to brown the top.

Sift the icing sugar and cinnamon together and sprinkle over the top. Serve warm or cold.

As an alternative
If you can't buy strudel-type pastry, use puff pastry instead. Roll it out thinly and treat the recipe as a two-crust pie — there's no need to brush between the layers.
Serves 8

BLUEBERRY CHOUX BUNS

Once you know you can make really successful choux pastry — and everyone can — you can mix and match endless sweet and savoury fillings. Use either your contact grill or your sandwich maker.

For the pastry

    40 g (1½ oz) butter
    125 ml (4 fl oz) water
    50 g (2 oz) flour
    a pinch of salt
    2 large eggs, lightly beaten
    sifted icing sugar, to decorate

For the filling

    150 ml (¼ pint) double cream
    60 ml (4 tablespoons) blueberry pie filling

Heat the butter and water in a pan until it boils. Tip in the flour and salt and beat for a couple of minutes until the mixture blends into a smooth paste.

Take the pan from the heat and beat in the eggs one at a time. Beat until the mixture is smooth and glossy.

Whip the cream for the filling. When it is stiff, stir in the pie filling.

Contact grill

Heat the grill to High. Grease the baking tray if necessary. Using two tablespoons, spoon the mixture on to the tray in eight heaps. Bake for about 15 minutes. The buns should be puffed up and a good brown colour. Split them at once and leave them on a rack to cool.

Sandwich maker

Heat the appliance and brush the plates with melted butter. Cook four or eight buns at a time. Check after 8 minutes, when they should be crisp and deep brown. Split them with a knife and leave to cool.

Just before serving, fill the buns with the blueberry cream. Dust them with plenty of icing sugar.

For a change
Flavour the cream filling with *thick* fresh fruit purée, sweetened or not. Strawberry, redcurrant, and raspberry are all delicious. But then so are apple purée spiced with cinnamon, and plum purée with a pinch of nutmeg.
Makes 8

SAVOURY CHOUX PUFFS

You can use either appliance for this recipe.

    1 recipe choux pastry (page 190)

For the filling
    40 g (1½ oz) butter
    40 g (1½ oz) flour
    300 ml (½ pint) milk
    60 ml (4 tablespoons) double cream
    225 g (8 oz) canned tuna fish, drained and flaked
    50 g (2 oz) Cheddar cheese, grated
    a pinch of cayenne
    salt and freshly ground black pepper
    a few drops of Tabasco sauce (optional)
    15 ml (1 tablespoon) chopped parsley

Make the choux puffs as described on page 190, split them and leave them to cool.

For the filling, melt the butter in a pan, stir in the flour and gradually pour on the milk. Stir until the sauce thickens, then simmer for 3 minutes. Remove from the heat, beat with a wooden spoon and cool.

Beat in the cream and stir in the remaining ingredients. Fill the buns just before serving.

As an alternative

When cooking on a contact grill, put the paste in small 5 ml (1 teaspoon) heaps to make bite-sized puffs. Fill them with the tuna mixture if you like, or with cream or cottage cheese flavoured with herbs. They make super snacks to have with drinks.

For a change

Vary the 'thick white sauce' filling with ideas of your own — minced cooked chicken and chopped walnuts; chopped hard-boiled egg, prawns and chives; cooked smoked haddock and chopped fennel are examples.

Makes 8

LARGE PIZZA

You can make an authentic pizza with yeast dough, or a quick version with scone dough. Quicker still, you can buy unadorned pizza dough frozen, and add your own choice of toppings and fillings.

Yeast dough

 25 g (1 oz) fresh yeast
 a pinch of sugar
 about 300 ml (½ pint) lukewarm water
 450 g (1 lb) white bread flour
 2.5 ml (½ teaspoon) salt
 45 ml (3 tablespoons) vegetable oil

Cream the yeast with the sugar, then pour on a little of the water to make a thin paste. Leave in a warm place for 15 minutes until it starts frothing.

 Measure off 25 g (1 oz) of the flour and set it aside. Sift the rest with the salt into a warm bowl. Pour in the yeast and oil. Mix thoroughly and knead to make a smooth, crack-free dough. (A food processor or electric mixer with a dough hook does the job in seconds.)

Form the dough into a ball, sprinkle it with some of the reserved flour, cover the bowl and leave in a warm place for 1½ − 2 hours, until it is twice the size.

Turn the dough out on to a floured board and knead it again. Shape it into a round and pinch up the edge to make a slightly raised rim. Place it on the baking dish.

Scone dough
   225 g (8 oz) self-raising flour
   5 ml (1 teaspoon) baking powder
   2.5 ml (½ teaspoon) salt
   1.5 ml (¼ teaspoon) freshly ground black pepper
   2.5 ml (½ teaspoon) mixed dried herbs
   40 g (1½ oz) butter
   150 ml (¼ pint) milk

Sift together the flour, baking powder, salt and pepper and stir in the herbs. Rub in the butter and mix to a soft dough with the milk. Knead lightly and roll out to about 2.5 cm (1 in) thick. Shape the dough to a round and put it on the baking dish.

Filling
   450 g (1 lb) tomatoes, skinned and sliced
   2.5 ml (½ teaspoon) dried basil
   2.5 ml (½ teaspoon) salt
   1.5 ml (¼ teaspoon) freshly ground black pepper
   5 ml (1 teaspoon) sugar
   225 g (8 oz) Cheddar cheese, grated
   can anchovy fillets, drained
   12 stuffed olives

Arrange the tomato slices to cover the dough, season them with the basil, salt, pepper and sugar and cover with cheese.

Make a lattice pattern with the anchovies and put olives in the spaces.

Bake the yeast or scone-dough pizza for about 15 minutes, until the base is firm and the topping brown and bubbly. Serve very hot.

For a change
There's no end to the possibilities in a pizza. To the base of tomatoes you can add strips of salami, bacon or ham; sliced mushrooms, red and green peppers, drained canned artichoke hearts or pimento; canned sweetcorn kernels, mussels, smoked oysters, shrimps, prawns — as you will.
Serves 4

PIZZA POCKETS

Calling all sandwich-maker owners! Here's a pizza version specially for you. Choose between fresh or frozen yeast dough, or scone dough. Roll it out thinly and cut it to fit your sandwich plates. On half the dough pieces arrange a filling of tomato slices, grated cheese plus your favourite flavouring (see list of ideas above. Top the dough shapes with a lid and press to seal the edges.

Sandwich maker
Heat the appliance. Brush the plates with melted butter. Cook the 'pizza pockets' for about 6 minutes for yeast dough, 5 minutes for scone dough. Top the pizzas with grated cheese and serve hot.

Contact grill
Heat the grill to High. Brush the pizza tops with melted butter, place in the baking dish and cook for about 10 − 12 minutes.
Makes 4 mini pizzas

SWEET PIZZAS

It's such a good idea, it's a shame to waste it. Here's the sweet version of 'pizza pockets'. Use either yeast or scone dough.

  1 recipe yeast or scone dough (page 192 or 193)
  8 ripe plums, halved and stoned
  2 cooking apples, peeled, cored and sliced
  8 – 16 dried dates (according to size), chopped
  2 small bananas, sliced
  soft light brown sugar, to serve
  150 ml (¼ pint) soured cream or plain yoghurt, to serve

Roll out the dough as described on pages 192 – 3 and cut into eight pieces. Divide the fruit between four pieces and top with the other four to make 'sandwiches'. Press the edges to seal.

Sandwich maker
Heat the appliance. Brush the plates with butter and cook the sweet pizzas for 6 minutes (yeast dough) or 5 minutes (scone dough).

Contact grill
Heat the grill to High.
   Brush the pizzas with melted butter and cook them for 10 – 12 minutes. Watch it! The filling gets mighty hot, especially if it includes dates. Sprinkle with brown sugar and serve with soured cream or yoghurt.

For a change
Ring the changes with other fruits in season — peaches, apricots, oranges. With soaked dried fruits — peaches or apricots again, pears, apple rings or prunes. And with drained, canned fruit or any frozen ones. You can use jam,

too. Try apricot jam with sliced bananas; strawberry jam with apple slices sprinkled with lemon juice, or blackcurrant jam with fresh pear slices.

Makes 4 mini pizzas

TOASTED MUESLI

Turn 'ordinary' muesli into the nutty, crunchy kind.

    30 ml (2 tablespoons) soft light brown sugar
    45 ml (3 tablespoons) clear honey
    350 g (12 oz) muesli cereal base
    40 ml (3 tablespoons) chopped mixed nuts, such as
        almonds, brazils, cashews, unsalted peanuts, walnuts
    5 ml (1 teaspoon) vanilla essence

Heat the contact grill to High.

Put the sugar and honey in the baking dish on a grill plate until it melts. Stir in the remaining ingredients and spread them evenly over the dish. Toast between the two grill plates, occasionally stirring with a wooden spoon, for about 15 minutes. Give a final stir to break up the clusters. Allow to cool thoroughly before storing in an airtight jar.

This makes a lovely breakfast background to added fruits — grated apple, sliced banana, strawberries, chopped dried dates, apricots or peaches, chopped candied peel, they're all delicious. Serve with plain yoghurt.

This quantity suits a baking dish 18.5 × 30 cm (7½ × 12 in). Toast it in two batches on a small appliance.

Makes about 450 g (1 lb)

PITTA BREAD

    275 g (10 oz) packet white bread mix
    185 ml (6½ fl oz) lukewarm water
    vegetable oil, for brushing

Tip the bread mix into a bowl, pour on the water and mix to a dough. Turn on to a lightly-floured board and knead for 5 minutes, until the dough is pliable. Form into a round and wrap loosely in oiled polythene. Leave in a warm place (top of cooker, airing cupboard) for about 45 minutes, until the dough has doubled in size. Turn on to the board again and knead for 1 minute more.

Heat the contact grill to High.

Divide the dough into six pieces and roll them out to about 10 × 23 cm (4 × 9 in). Press the corners to make the traditional oval shape. Brush the pittas with oil on both sides and grill them, one or two at a time, between the grill plates, for 2 minutes. Turn them and grill for 1 minute more. As you cook the pittas, wrap them in a tea towel to keep them warm.

Split them and fill with meat, fish or vegetable kebabs, or cut them in slices and use them as 'dunks' for savoury dips.

As an alternative
Make wholewheat pittas, using brown bread mix.
Makes 6 pittas

DEVONSHIRE SPLITS

For both your appliances.

> 275 g (10 oz) packet white bread mix
> 25 g (1 oz) butter
> 25 g (1 oz) caster sugar
> 1 egg
> 150 ml (¼ pint) lukewarm milk

For the filling
> 150 ml (¼ pint) double cream, whipped
> strawberry or raspberry jam
> icing sugar, for dusting

Tip the bread mix into a bowl, rub in the butter and stir in the sugar. Beat the egg and milk together, pour on to the dry ingredients and mix to a dough. Turn on to a lightly-floured board and knead for 5 minutes, until it is elastic. Cover the dough loosely in oiled polythene and leave in a warm place for about 45 minutes, to 'prove'. It should double in size.

Contact grill
Heat the appliance to High. Grease the baking dish.

Divide the dough into eight pieces and shape into long flat buns. Place them on the baking dish and bake, between the grill plates, for 8 − 10 minutes, until they have risen and sound hollow when tapped.

Leave them on a wire rack to cool.

Split the buns lengthways and fill them with cream and jam.

Dust them with icing sugar.

Sandwich maker
Heat the appliance.

Divide the dough into twelve pieces. Brush the plates with oil and cook for about 4 minutes, until the buns are light and puffy. Cool on a wire rack, then split and fill them and dust with icing sugar.

For a change
Make spiced buns, à la Hot Cross Bun, by adding 7.5 ml (1½ teaspoons) mixed spice, a pinch of grated nutmeg, 50 g (2 oz) currants and 25 g (1 oz) sultanas to the dry ingredients.
Makes 8 − 12 buns

9 Puddings

Creamy egg custard shivering over a layer of peaches; old-fashioned rice pudding like mother used to make; strawberry shortcake, a triumph of the soft-fruit season; grilled fresh pineapple with a luscious coconut meringue topping; dairy-rich cheesecake ready in only half an hour — all things are possible, and in a fraction of the time.

All these puddings and many more — baked suet sponges and fruit crumbles, too — can be cooked on a contact grill. Use the baking dish as a *bain marie* with a little water and you can make the most delicate of egg custards, with no fear of scorching or curdling. Sprinkle sugar on the top, pop it back under the grill plate and you have that most luxurious of desserts, *crème brûlée*.

The main point to remember is that you must never over-fill the baking dish, or any other dish, especially with a mixture that is going to rise.

Measure the actual cooking area of your appliance, collect together the baking dishes, flan rings and ovenproof dishes that fit it and keep them close by, at the ready when you need them. It's infuriating if it takes longer to retrieve a dish from the back of the cupboard than it does to make a pudding! If necessary, invest gradually in more dishes specially chosen to fit your contact grill. Sandwich rings and flan rings that are too large for the grill plates result in puddings perfect in every respect but one — they'll have uncooked edges.

The restriction of height between the grill plates is a

challenge that's easily met. If, for example, you want to make a cheesecake with a meringue topping, the two layers into the one space won't go. But it takes only a moment to 'seal' a meringue topping, so shape it on non-stick paper, pop it under the grill and then transfer it to its rightful place — the chocolate pudding on page 219 is an example of this technique.

Fresh fruit, packed with vitamins and valuable dietary fibre, makes perfect hot puddings, sticky with honey or moist brown sugar and aromatic with spices. A medley of grilled fruits (page 224) gives a new meaning to the term 'fruit salad' and gives you the chance to present a lavish-looking pudding in moments.

Custards, sponges, crumbles, pastry, baked and grilled fruits — with such a selection, who needs an oven!

If you have a sandwich maker and not a contact grill, don't — please — bypass this chapter. It's packed with ideas for sweet pastry fillings, pot pourris of fruits, nuts and spices that you can mix and match with the 'sandwich bakes' in the previous chapter.

PEACH BRÛLÉE

> 2 large, ripe peaches, skinned, halved, stoned and sliced,
>   or 2 canned peaches, drained and sliced
> 2 egg yolks
> 1 whole egg
> 100 g (4 oz) caster sugar
> a few drops of vanilla essence
> 300 ml (½ pint) milk, warm

Heat the grill to High.

Divide the sliced peaches between six small flameproof ramekin dishes. Beat the egg yolks, the egg, half the sugar and the vanilla essence together, then pour on the warm milk. Beat well and pour into the six dishes.

Pour about 2.5 cm (1 in) water into the baking dish and stand the ramekins in it. Cover the dish with foil and cook between the grill plates for 10 minutes.

Remove the dishes from the water, dry them and stand them on the grill plate. Sprinkle the remaining sugar over the custards and grill, uncovered, for 3 minutes. Transfer the dishes to a rack to cool, then chill them in the refrigerator.

Serve chilled, with cream.

For a change
Other fruits are just as delicious — try sliced strawberries, orange segments, bananas. And for a special treat, replace all or half the milk with single cream.

Use the extra egg whites to make meringues, or a meringue topping.
Serves 6

RASPBERRY CUSTARD PUDDING

    450 g (1 lb) raspberries
    45 ml (3 tablespoons) caster sugar (vanilla sugar (see note) if possible)
    15 ml (1 tablespoon) flour
    2 eggs
    300 ml (½ pint) soured cream

Heat the grill to High.

Put the raspberries and 30 ml (2 tablespoons) of the sugar into an 850 ml (1½ pint) baking dish. Heat between the grill plates for 3 minutes while you make the custard.

Put the flour into a bowl and beat in the eggs until the mixture is smooth. Beat in the remaining sugar and then, gradually, the soured cream. Pour the custard over the fruit and bake for about 10 minutes, until the custard is just set. It should shake like a jelly when the dish is moved from side to side.

The pudding is a glorious treat served hot, but can also be enjoyed cold. In this case, leave it to cool, then chill in the refrigerator.

For a change
Vanilla sugar gives a subtle and natural flavour to many puddings — and to baked goods, too. Just store a vanilla pod in a jar of sugar and top it up with more sugar as needed. You can use a spray of fresh or dried bay leaves or a sprig of rosemary in the same way.

CHERRY CLAFOUTIE

The English and the French have argued for years over who invented this scrumptious pudding. But I know who first thought of grilling it!

      100 g (4 oz) *plain* flour
      5 ml (1 teaspoon) salt
      2 eggs
      200 ml (7 fl oz) milk
      25 g (1 oz) caster sugar
      5 ml (1 teaspoon) vegetable oil
      350 g (12oz) cherries, stoned, or use pitted canned cher-
         ries, drained
      30 ml (2 tablespoons) demerara sugar, to decorate

Heat the grill to High.
      Sift together the flour and salt, break in the eggs one at a time and beat. Slowly pour on the milk, beating until the mixture forms a smooth paste. Stir in the sugar and oil.

Put the cherries into an 850 ml (1½ pint) baking dish and pour on the batter. Cook for 15 — 20 minutes, until the batter is crispy. Sprinkle on the sugar and serve hot, with soured or whipped cream.

This quantity is for a baking dish 18.5 × 30 cm (7½ × 12 in). If yours is smaller, reduce the ingredients proportionately. It doesn't do to overcrowd the dish. There's nowhere for the batter to rise and it will spill over.

For a change
Fresh cherries enjoy only a very brief season, and canned ones (I don't know why) are expensive. So adapt this recipe for use with other fruits — sliced cooking apples, peaches, apricots, or soaked dried fruits. Don't use rhubarb – it's too weepy, and dilutes the batter.
Serves 4 — 6

VANILLA CHEESECAKE

Once you know you can bake a perfect cheesecake on your contact grill, the whole lovely world of these rich, creamy confections is before you — just adapt your other favourite recipes.

50 g (2 oz) butter
225 g (8 oz) shortbread biscuits, crushed
2.5 ml (½ teaspoon) ground cinnamon
a pinch of grated nutmeg

For the filling
175 g (6 oz) cream cheese
175 g (6 oz) cottage cheese
2 large eggs
15 ml (1 tablespoon) sultanas

    5 ml (1 teaspoon) vanilla essence
    100 g (4oz) caster sugar (use vanilla sugar (page 202) if
       you have it)

For the topping
    150 ml (5 fl oz) soured cream
    50 g (2 oz) caster sugar (or vanilla sugar)
    a few drops of vanilla essence
    grated nutmeg, to decorate

Heat the grill to High. Grease an 18 cm (7 in) sandwich tin.

Put the butter in a small pan and stand it on the grill plate.
When the butter has melted, stir in the biscuit crumbs and
spices. Turn the mixture into the tin and press it down
firmly.

To make the filling, beat the cheeses together, then beat in
the eggs one at a time. Stir in the sultanas, vanilla essence
and sugar. Pour into the crumb case and bake for about 30
minutes. To check if the filling is set, insert a knife — it should
come out clean. Leave the cheesecake to cool while you make
the topping.

Beat the soured cream, sugar and vanilla essence together.
Spread over the cooled cheesecake and sprinkle with grated
nutmeg to decorate.
Serves 8

LEMON PAVLOVA

For the lightest, dreamiest pudding, a 'marshmallow'
meringue with a tangy filling that's less rich, less fattening
than cream.

    3 egg whites
    a pinch of salt
    175 g (6 oz) granulated sugar
    5 ml (1 teaspoon) vanilla essence

5 ml (1 teaspoon) distilled white vinegar
10 ml (2 teaspoons) cornflour
2 − 3 thin slices of lemon, halved, to decorate

For the filling
1 whole egg
75 g (3 oz) caster sugar
grated rind and juice of 2 lemons
2 egg whites

Heat the grill to Medium.

Whisk the egg whites with the salt until they are stiff enough to stand in peaks. Gradually add the sugar, still whisking, until the mixture is firm and stiff. Stir in the vanilla essence, vinegar and cornflour. Line the baking dish with vegetable parchment paper and spread out the meringue mixture. Level the top and check that it comes below the rim of the dish − close-contact-grilled pavlova is a sticky business!

Cook for about 15 minutes, or until the meringue is pale brown and crisp outside. It should be soft inside. Remove from the heat, cool and then peel off the backing paper.

While the meringue is cooling, make the filling. Put the egg, lemon rind, lemon juice and sugar into a bowl. Pour some warm water into the baking dish, place on the grill and stand the bowl in the water. Whisk until the mixture thickens, then remove from the heat and allow to cool. Switch off the appliance.

Whisk the egg whites until they are stiff, then fold them into the lemon mixture. Pour the filling into the meringue case. Decorate with the lemon slices.

For a change
Obviously whipped cream and fresh, frozen or canned fruits may be used to fill the pavlova case. But this 'lemon meringue pie' filling is refreshingly different.
Serves 6

OLD-FASHIONED RICE PUDDING

    50 g (2 oz) short-grain rice
    600 ml (1 pint) milk
    15 ml (1 tablespoon) soft light brown sugar
    30 ml (2 tablespoons) sultanas
    freshly grated nutmeg

Put the rice, milk, sugar and sultanas into an 850 ml (1½ pint) baking dish, stir well and leave for about 30 minutes. Sprinkle the top with nutmeg.

Heat the grill to Medium. Cover the dish with foil and cook for about 15 — 20 minutes, or until the rice is tender and has absorbed most of the milk.

Do cover the top with foil. I forgot once and it took ages to clean splashed-up, burned-on milk from the top plate.

BREAD AND BUTTER PUDDING

    8 thin slices of bread and butter, cut from a small loaf
      (crusts removed)
    45 ml (3 tablespoons) currants
    30 ml (2 tablespoons) chopped mixed candied peel
    425 ml (¾ pint) milk
    2 egg yolks
    1 whole egg
    15 — 30 ml (1 — 2 tablespoons) sugar
    30 ml (2 tablespoons) sweet sherry

Grease an 850 ml (1½ pint) baking dish. Arrange layers of bread, buttered side up, sprinkled with currants and peel. Beat together the milk, egg yolks, whole egg, sugar and sherry and pour over the bread. Leave the dish to stand for at least 30 minutes.

Heat the grill to High. Bake the pudding for about 10 minutes, until the top is crisp and brown. Serve hot.
Serves 4 — 6

QUEEN OF PUDDINGS

50 g (2 oz) breadcrumbs
25 g (1 oz) caster sugar
grated rind of 1 lemon
300 ml (½ pint) milk, boiling
25 g (1 oz) butter
2 egg yolks, lightly beaten
30 ml (2 tablespoons) raspberry jam, warmed

For the topping
2 egg whites
75 g (3 oz) caster sugar

Put the breadcrumbs into a bowl and stir in the sugar and lemon rind. Pour on the milk, stir in the butter and set aside for 15 minutes. Stir in the egg yolks.

Heat the grill to High. Grease an 850 ml (1½ pint) baking dish.

Pour in the pudding mixture, cover with foil and bake for about 12 — 15 minutes.

Meanwhile, whisk the egg whites until they form peaks then fold in the sugar. Remove the pudding from the grill. Spread the jam over the top and cover it with the meringue. Smooth the top and check that the top grill plate will not quite touch it.

Return the pudding to the grill and cook for a further 3 minutes, just to 'set' the meringue. Serve hot.

APRICOT TART

An 'ordinary' shortcrust with a difference — an orange flavour — which can be made in both your appliances.

    350 g (12 oz) dried apricots, soaked
    50 g (2 oz) soft light brown sugar
    300 ml (½ pint) soured cream
    15 ml (1 tablespoon) toasted almonds

For the pastry
    175 g (6 oz) margarine
    225 g (8 oz) flour
    grated rind and juice of 1 orange

Cook the apricots and sugar with just enough of the soaking water to cover them, until they are tender. This takes about 50 minutes in a pan on the cooker, 15 minutes in the baking dish on the contact grill. (Cover the dish with foil.) Reserve four apricots for decoration and purée the rest in a blender. Leave to cool.

To make the pastry, rub the margarine into the flour, stir in the orange rind and bind with the orange juice. Wrap the dough in film or foil and chill for 30 minutes.

Roll out the pastry.

Contact grill
Heat the grill to High. Grease a 20 cm (7½ in) flan ring on a baking sheet with margarine or butter. Line with the pastry and prick the base with a fork. Cover with foil and dried beans (about 6 tablespoons) and bake 'blind' in this way for about 12 minutes. Remove the foil and beans (see page 180) and cook for a further 3 minutes.

Pour the cooled apricot purée into the flan case. Top with the soured cream and cook for another 3 — 4 minutes. Allow to cool, then decorate with the reserved apricots, halved, and the almonds.

Sandwich maker

Heat the appliance.

Cut the pastry to fit the sandwich plates. Brush the edges of half the shapes with milk. Spoon the apricot purée into the centre of these pieces and top it with a spoonful of soured cream. Put on the pastry lids and press down the edges. Brush the sandwich plates with butter, put the fruit pies in place and cook for about 6 minutes, or until the pastry is nicely browned.

If there is any apricot purée left, thin it with a little lemon juice and serve it separately, with the remaining soured cream.

CRUNCHY MINCEMEAT FLAN

150 g (5 oz) wholewheat flour
1.5 ml (¼ teaspoon) salt
75 g (3 oz) margarine
1 egg yolk
15 ml (1 tablespoon) water
225 g (8 oz) mincemeat

For the topping
40 g (1½ oz) soft margarine
25 g (1 oz) soft dark brown sugar
75 g (3 oz) rolled porridge oats
grated rind and juice of 1 orange

Heat the grill to High. Grease an 18 cm (7 in) flan ring and a baking sheet.

Mix together the flour and salt and rub in the margarine to make fine 'breadcrumbs'. Mix the egg yolk and water and stir into the dry ingredients to make a stiff dough. Turn out and knead until the dough is smooth and free of cracks. Wrap in film or foil and chill for about 1 hour.

Roll out the pastry and lift it into the flan ring. Trim the edges and prick the base with a fork. Spread the mincemeat in the pastry case and level it out.

For the topping, cream the margarine and sugar, stir in the oats, orange rind and orange juice. Spread over the mincemeat and level the top.

Bake for 15 minutes, then lower the heat to Medium. Bake for about another 10 minutes, until the top is crisp and golden brown. Serve hot or cold.
Serves 6

KOLAC

What is it? It's an East European pudding, sticky and rich, which is served cold, topped with chilled soured cream. It can be made in either the contact grill or sandwich maker.

>   225 g (8 oz) wholewheat flour
>   10 ml (2 teaspoons) baking powder
>   1.5 ml (¼ teaspoon) salt
>   100 g (4 oz) butter
>   75 g (3 oz) soft light brown sugar
>   2.5 ml (½ teaspoon) mixed spice
>   1 egg, beaten
>   150 ml (¼ pint) soured cream

For the topping
>   2 bananas, mashed
>   175 g (6 oz) dried stoned dates, chopped
>   350 g (12 oz) cottage cheese, sieved
>   25 g (1 oz) demerara sugar
>   25 g (1 oz) butter

Sift the flour, baking powder and salt into a bowl and stir in the bran left behind in the sieve. Rub in the butter until the mixture is like crumbs, then stir in the sugar and mixed spice. Mix to a soft dough with the egg and roll out the paste thinly.

Contact grill

Heat the grill to High. Grease a Swiss roll tin 23 × 30 cm (9 × 12 in). Or, on a small appliance, bake in two batches.

Lift the pastry on to the tin. Spread it evenly with the mashed banana and scatter on the dates. Carefully spread on the sieved cheese to cover the top completely, without leaving any gaps. Sprinkle with the demerara sugar and flake the butter over the top.

Bake for about 15 minutes, until the pastry is cooked and the topping is bubbly. Allow to cool, then cut in squares.

Serve each slice topped with a blob of soured cream. If you like, sprinkle on a little mixed spice to decorate.

Sandwich maker

Heat the appliance.

Cut the pastry to fit your sandwich plates. It should make twelve pieces. Brush the edges of half of them with milk. Divide the mashed banana, dates and cheese between six pastry shapes, sprinkle with demerara sugar and press the pastry lids in place. Do not overfill the 'pasties' or they will burst in cooking — and burning dates are a sticky mess.

Brush the sandwich plates with butter, put the pies in place and cook for about 6 minutes, or until the pastry is crisp. Allow the pastries to cool. Serve them with soured cream.

For a change

An alternative version of this recipe uses two dessert apples, peeled, cored and chopped instead of the dates.

Serves 6

STRAWBERRY SHORTCAKE

A perfect summer pudding — and you don't have to stifle yourself by switching on the oven to make it.

225 g (8 oz) flour
10 ml (2 teaspoons) baking powder
2.5 ml (½ teaspoon) salt
7.5 ml (1½ teaspoons) mixed spice
75 g (3 oz) caster sugar
100 g (4 oz) butter
75 g (3 oz) chopped walnuts
2 small egg yolks
about 75 ml (5 tablespoons) milk

For the topping
350 g (12 oz) strawberries, hulled
25 g (1 oz) caster sugar
150 ml (¼ pint) double cream, whipped
1 egg white, stiffly beaten

Heat the grill to High. Grease two 18 cm (7 in) sandwich tins or two flan rings and a baking sheet.

Sift the flour, baking powder, salt and spice and stir in the sugar. Rub in the butter until it is like fine crumbs. Stir in the walnuts. Mix together the egg and milk and stir into the nut mixture to make a soft dough. Stop before the dough becomes sticky — you might not need all the milk.

Turn the dough on to a board lightly dusted with flour and knead until there are no more cracks. Divide the dough in half. Put one half in each tin and press it to cover the base evenly. Prick with a fork.

Bake for about 10 minutes, or until the shortcake is golden brown. Turn it out on to a wire rack to cool. Bake the second piece of dough in the same way.

For the filling and topping, halve the strawberries if they are large and sprinkle them with the sugar. Fold the whisked egg white into the cream. Reserve a few strawberries for decoration. Fold the others into the cream.

Use half the cream to sandwich the two shortcake layers

together. Spread the remainder on top and decorate with the
reserved strawberries.
Serves 6

FRUIT CROÛTES

It couldn't be simpler — an 'open sandwich' of bread topped
with fruit and baked in moments.

    4 slices of bread, about 2 cm (¾ in) thick, buttered on
        both sides
    50 — 75 g (2 — 3 oz) demerara sugar
    12 dessert plums or greengages, halved and stoned
    25 g (1 oz) butter

Heat the grill to High.

Cut the bread slices into 10 cm (4 in) circles (the exact size
isn't critical). Arrange the bread rounds in the baking dish,
greased if necessary. Sprinkle the bread with half the sugar.

Arrange the fruit in a single layer, cut sides up, on the
bread, sprinkle with the remaining sugar and dot with pieces
of butter. Bake for about 10 minutes, until the bread is crisp
and the fruit bubbling. Serve hot sprinkled with more
crunchy demerara sugar, with cream or soured cream.

For a change
Other fruits are good a-top toasty bread. Brush halved, ripe
apricots or peaches with lemon juice to preserve their colour.

BAKED FRUIT SANDWICH

    450 g (1 lb) blackcurrants
    60 ml (4 tablespoons) water
    100 g (4 oz) sugar

   8 thin slices of bread and butter, cut from a large loaf
      (crusts removed)
   2.5 ml (½ teaspoon) ground cinnamon

Heat the grill to High.

Put the blackcurrants in the baking dish with the water and half the sugar. Cook between the grill plates until the sugar has dissolved and the fruit softens — about 4 minutes. Drain the fruit thoroughly — the juice can be diluted for a delicious drink or used, for example, to flavour baked apples.

Rinse the baking dish and, if necessary, grease it with oil or margarine. Line the base of the dish with half the bread and butter slices, buttered sides up. Cover them with the fruit and then with the remaining bread slices, buttered sides up. Mix the remaining sugar with the cinnamon and sprinkle it over the bread. Flatten the top slightly with your hand.

Bake for about 12 minutes, until the topping is crisp and crackly. The underneath layer, by scrumptious contrast, will be moist and fruit-flavoured.

This quantity works well in a baking dish 18.5 × 30 cm (7½ × 12 in). For a smaller one, reduce the number of bread slices accordingly. The top grill plate shouldn't touch the sugary layer. If it does, you have a sticky mess to clear up.

For a change
Try cherries.

As an alternative
You can use thin slices of slightly stale sponge cake, or trifle sponges.
Serves 6

PLUM CRUMBLE

   50 g (2 oz) soft brown sugar
   2.5 ml (½ teaspoon) ground cinnamon
   450 g (1 lb) plums, halved and stoned

For the topping
- 100 g (4 oz) flour
- 100 g (4 oz) rolled porridge oats
- 5 ml (1 teaspoon) ground cinnamon
- 100 g (4 oz) margarine
- 50 g (2 oz) demerara sugar

Heat the grill to High.

Mix the sugar and cinnamon. Put the plums in a 1 litre (2 pint) dish, sprinkle with the spiced sugar and stir.

Mix together the flour, oats and cinnamon, rub in the margarine and stir in the sugar. Sprinkle the crumble topping over the fruit. Cover the dish with foil.

Bake for about 15 minutes. Even through the foil, the topping should be crisp and brown. Serve hot or cold.

For a change
Fruit crumbles are a great success on the grill – the heat from the lower plate cooks the fruit to perfection without cooking it to a mash. Try other combinations as the seasons change — rhubarb and ginger, gooseberry, cherry, mixed summer fruits, apple and blackberry, they are all delicious.

Using a small appliance, reduce the ingredients proportionately and use a smaller dish. It shouldn't be over-full. *Serves 4 – 6*

RHUBARB AND GINGER CRUMBLE

Even quicker to make than the 'rubbed in' crumble topping, and a good way to use unwanted bread, this topping can be used with other seasonal fruits.

30 ml (2 tablespoons) golden syrup

grated rind and juice of 1 orange
25 g (1 oz) soft light brown sugar
450 g (1 lb) rhubarb, cut into 2.5 cm (1 in) pieces
2 pieces preserved ginger, sliced

For the topping
75 g (3 oz) butter, melted
50 g (2 oz) soft light brown sugar
175 g (6 oz) breadcrumbs, white or wholewheat (not packet crumbs)
5 ml (1 teaspoon) ground ginger

Heat the grill to High.

Heat the treacle, orange rind, orange juice and sugar in the baking dish until the treacle melts. Stir in the rhubarb and sliced ginger.

For the topping, melt the butter and sugar and stir in the breadcrumbs and ginger. Spread the topping over the fruit, cover with foil and bake for about 15 minutes. The topping should be crisp. Serve hot or cold.

This quantity fits a baking dish 18.5 × 30 cm (7½ × 12 in). Reduce the ingredients proportionately for a smaller one. The rhubarb juice will spill over if the dish is too full. *Serves 4 — 6*

APPLE AND WALNUT BETTY

50 g (2 oz) butter
175 g (6 oz) breadcrumbs (not packet crumbs)
100 g (4 oz) chopped walnuts
50 g (2 oz) demerara sugar
450 g (1 lb) cooking apples, peeled, cored and sliced
30 ml (2 tablespoons) lemon juice
50 g (2 oz) raisins
1 red-skinned dessert apple, to decorate

Heat the grill to High.

Melt the butter in the baking dish, stir in the bread-crumbs, walnuts and sugar and cook between the grill plates, stirring occasionally, until the crumbs are dry — about 4 minutes. Tip the crumbs from the dish.

Toss the apple slices in lemon juice and mix them with the raisins. Spread a layer of crumbs in the dish, then apples, more crumbs and so on, finishing with crumbs. Cover the dish with foil and bake for about 12 — 15 minutes, until the apples are tender — pierce the top with a skewer or sharp knife to test.

Core and slice the dessert apple, toss it in lemon juice and arrange the slices to decorate the pudding top. Serve hot or cold.

This quantity suits a baking dish 18.5 × 30 cm (7½ × 12 in). For a smaller one, use smaller quantities.

As an alternative
Copy the idea — layers of fruit and crumbs — with other fruits. Rhubarb is specially good.
Serves 4 — 6

DUTCH APPLE STREUSEL

150 g (5 oz) butter
225 g (8 oz) flour
5 ml (1 teaspoon) baking powder
5 ml (1 teaspoon) caster sugar
1 egg yolk
60 ml (4 tablespoons) milk
350 g (12 oz) cooking apples, peeled, cored and thinly sliced

For the topping
   40 g (1½ oz) butter
   50 g (2 oz) flour
   50 g (2 oz) soft light brown sugar
   5 ml (1 teaspoon) grated orange rind

Heat the grill to High. Grease an 18 cm (7½ in) shallow cake tin.

Cream the butter to soften it. Sift together the flour and baking powder and beat them into the butter. Stir in the sugar. Beat the egg yolk and milk together and stir into the dry ingredients. Turn the mixture into the tin and level the top.

Arrange the sliced apples in neat rows or circles.

For the topping, rub the butter into the flour and stir in the sugar and orange rind. Sprinkle on the apples.

Bake for about 15 — 18 minutes, or until the cake is firm and the topping is golden brown. Serve hot or warm.

A really lovely accompaniment is whipped cream stirred with a little clear honey.
Serves 6

BAKED PEAR SPONGE

   100 g (4 oz) self-raising flour
   7.5 ml (1½ teaspoons) ground ginger
   50 g (2 oz) shredded suet
   50 g (2 oz) demerara sugar
   1 large egg
   about 30 ml (2 tablespoons) milk

For the fruit layer
   450 g (1 lb) dessert pears, peeled, cored and sliced
   50 g (2 oz) demerara sugar
   40 g (1½ oz) seedless raisins
   2.5 ml (½ teaspoon) ground ginger

Heat the grill to High. Grease an 850 ml (1½ pint) flame-proof dish.

Sift together the flour and ground ginger and stir in the suet and sugar. Beat in the egg and add just enough milk to give a soft mixture.

Mix together the pears, sugar, raisins and ginger and arrange them in the base of the dish. Pour on the sponge mixture and level the top. Bake for about 15 minutes, until the pudding has a good crisp crust. Serve hot.

BAKED CHOCOLATE PUD

75 g (3 oz) self-raising flour
25 g (1 oz) cocoa powder
50 g (2 oz) shredded suet
50 g (2 oz) caster sugar (use vanilla sugar (page 202) if you
    have it)
a few drops of vanilla essence
2 egg yolks
45 ml (3 tablespoons) milk

For the sauce
15 g (½ oz) butter
100 g (4 oz) bitter chocolate, broken into pieces
15 ml (1 tablespoon) milk

For the topping
2 egg whites
75 g (3 oz) caster sugar
15 ml (1 tablespoon) granulated sugar

Heat the grill to High. Grease an 850 ml (1½ pint) baking dish.

Sift together the flour and cocoa and stir in the suet, sugar and vanilla essence. Beat in the egg yolks and milk. Turn the mixture into the dish and level the top. Bake for about 15 minutes, until the pudding is well risen and has a firm crust.

While the pudding is cooking, put the butter, broken chocolate pieces and milk into a small pan and melt it. Beat the sauce until it is smooth and shiny and pour it over the pudding. Keep the pudding warm.

The meringue topping won't fit on top of the pudding and under the grill, but it's an easy matter to make it separately and transfer it. Whisk the egg whites until they are stiff. Fold in all the caster sugar.

Mark a piece of vegetable parchment paper with the outline of the pudding dish and put it in the baking tray. Spread the meringue mixture to fill the shape, sprinkle the granulated sugar on top and grill for 3 minutes. Lift the meringue off the paper and slide it on to the pudding — two fish slices make deft work of it. Serve hot.

BAKED GRAPEFRUIT SALAD

    4 grapefruits
    2 oranges
    50 g (2 oz) dried apricots, soaked and drained
    90 ml (6 tablespoons) medium sherry
    50 g (2 oz) soft light brown sugar
    50 g (2 oz) butter, melted

Peel the grapefruits and oranges, divide them into segments and discard the pips. Arrange the fruit in a baking dish in a single layer. Pour on the sherry and set aside for at least 30 minutes, for the flavour to be absorbed.

Heat the grill to High.

Sprinkle the sugar over the fruit and drip the butter over it. Cook for 5 — 8 minutes, until the fruit is piping hot and the top is sizzling. Serve hot, with chilled cream or, better still, ice cream.

As an alternative
Use marsala or one of the 'cheap' fruit wines, such as orange or apricot, in place of the sherry.

BAKED PEACHES

Here's a recipe that puts broken meringues to delectable use. It seems a shame to crush some specially, but actually it's really worth it!

40 g (1½ oz) butter
15 ml (1 tablespoon) icing sugar
60 ml (4 tablespoons) ground almonds
grated rind and juice of 2 oranges
2 meringue halves, crushed (page 172)
1 egg white, stiffly beaten
30 ml (2 tablespoons) clear honey
4 large, ripe peaches, halved and stoned

Heat the grill to High.
Beat the butter and sugar until creamy, then stir in the ground almonds, orange rind and crushed meringues. Fold in the egg white. Heat the honey and orange juice in the baking dish for a minute. Arrange the peach halves, cut sides up, in this sauce. Spoon on the filling and smooth the tops.
Cook for about 5 minutes, until the peaches are hot and the topping has a pale brown crust. Serve hot.

For a change
Try using similar tactics with very ripe plums. Halve and stone them, spread them in a single layer in the dish, cut sides up, then spread the filling evenly over the top.

As an alternative
In place of the meringues, crush two macaroons, or 50 g (2 oz) ratafias — but only if you enjoy a really pronounced almond flavour.

GINGERED PEARS

  4 large dessert pears
  60 ml (4 tablespoons) ginger marmalade
  75 g (3 oz) butter
  45 ml (3 tablespoons) ginger wine

Peel and halve the pears. Scrape out the cores — a teaspoon is good for this. Arrange the fruit in a baking dish, cut sides up, spoon the marmalade over them, and flake the butter over the top. Pour the ginger wine round the pears.
  Bake for about 10 minutes — or until the pears are tender — basting them frequently in the sauce.
  Serve very hot. Creamy ice cream is lovely with them.

BAKED APPLE CHEESE

A variation on a popular favourite.

  4 medium-sized cooking apples
  50 g (2 oz) soft light brown sugar
  100 g (4 oz) seedless raisins
  225 g (8 oz) cottage cheese
  grated rind and juice of 1 lemon

Heat the grill to High.

Core the apples but do not peel them. Cut them in half horizontally. Arrange them cut sides up, in a baking dish that just fits them — so that they stand upright.

Mix together the sugar, raisins, cottage cheese, lemon rind and lemon juice. Pile the mixture on the apple halves and smooth the top — the closed grill plates should not touch the topping.

Cook for about 10 minutes, or until the apples are just tender but not collapsing, and the topping is sticky. Serve hot.

COAT-COLLAR BANANAS

30 ml (2 tablespoons) blanched almonds, flaked
4 large, slightly under-ripe bananas
60 ml (4 tablespoons) rum or brandy butter

Heat the grill to High.

Spread the almonds in the baking tray and grill for 2 — 3 minutes, stirring occasionally, until they are deep brown. Tip them out and set aside.

Using the point of a sharp knife, make two parallel slits 12 mm (½ in) apart along the length of each banana skin, without piercing the fruit. Arrange the bananas in the baking tray and cook for about 10 minutes, until the skins have turned black.

Zip off the strip of skin from each banana, dot a little of the flavoured butter along the exposed line of fruit and top with the toasted almonds.

Serve the bananas hot, still in their jackets, with the rest of the flavoured butter separately.

As an alternative
You have no flavoured butter? Top the baked bananas with jam instead. Zip off the strip of skin, spoon a streak of jam

along the opening and pop under the grill for a couple of minutes. Top with the nuts. Apricot, quince or plum jam are all good.

GRILLED APPLE RINGS

60 ml (4 tablespoons) honey
25 g (1 oz) butter
a pinch of ground cloves
4 cooking apples, peeled, cored and cut into 12 mm (½ in) thick rings
1.5 ml (¼ teaspoon) ground cinnamon
30 ml (2 tablespoons) toasted almonds (page 223), chopped
150 ml (¼ pint) double cream, whipped

Heat the grill to High.

Put the honey, butter and ground cloves into a small pan and stand it on the grill to melt. Arrange the apple rings on the baking dish, brush them with the honey mixture and grill them for 5 minutes. Turn the apple slices over, brush them again and grill them until they are golden brown.

Arrange the apple slices on a heated serving dish and pour over any remaining honey sauce.

Stir the cinnamon and nuts into the cream and serve it separately.

GRILLED FRUIT SALAD

50 g (2 oz) soft dark brown sugar
2 cooking apples, peeled, cored and cut into 12 mm (½ in) thick rings
4 pineapple rings (they may be canned ones, well drained and dried)

4 — 8 apricots (according to size) halved and stoned (or use canned ones, drained)

25 g (1 oz) butter, melted

Heat the grill to High.

Put the brown sugar into a polythene bag, put in the fruit, a little at a time, and gently turn the bag from side to side to coat the fruit evenly with sugar.

Tip the fruit out of the bag and arrange in a single layer in the baking dish and drip the melted butter over it. Grill for about 5 minutes, turn the fruit and grill until the other side is sizzling and brown.

Serve the fruit very hot with ice cream for a stunning contrast.

GRILLED PINEAPPLE MERINGUES

A real 'party' piece, as impressive as it is quick.

25 g (1 oz) butter

6 slices pineapple, about 2.5 cm (1 in) thick — use fresh or canned

2 egg whites

100 g (4 oz) caster sugar

50 g (2 oz) desiccated coconut, plus a little extra to decorate

Heat the grill to High. Melt the butter in a small pan on a grill plate.

If the pineapple is canned, pat it really dry with kitchen paper. Brush the pineapple slices on both sides with butter and grill them 'in close contact' for 4 minutes.

Whisk the egg whites until they form peaks, add half the sugar and whisk to the same stage again. Mix the remaining sugar with the coconut and fold it into the meringue mixture, using a metal spoon.

Lift the top grill plate. Spoon the meringue over the pine-apple and smooth it flat — it mustn't touch the grill when it's back in position. Sprinkle on a little extra coconut. Grill the meringue for 2 — 3 minutes, until it browns. Serve at once. *Serves 6*

PARADISE BANANAS

> 25 g (1 oz) butter
> 15 ml (1 tablespoon) honey
> 15 ml (1 tablespoon) lemon juice
> 30 ml (2 tablespoons) rum
> 2 egg whites
> 75 g (3 oz) caster sugar
> 25 g (1 oz) semolina
> 25 g (1 oz) mini chocolate drops
> 4 bananas, peeled

Heat the grill to High.

Melt the butter, honey, limon juice and rum in a baking dish on the grill plate. Whisk the egg whites until they form snowy peaks and add 50 g (2 oz) of the sugar. Whisk back to the 'peaky' stage. With a metal spoon, fold in the rest of the sugar, the semolina and the chocolate drops.

Slit the bananas lengthways and arrange them in the baking dish. Spoon over the rum sauce. Spread the meringue out on top. Cook for 8 — 10 minutes, until the sauce sizzles and the meringue topping is very brown. Serve hot with lashings of cream.

For a change
Try cooking apples like this — it's quick, easy and delicious. Peel, core and very thinly slice two large cooking apples; they just love the rum sauce!

CARIBBEAN MERINGUE

This is a brown meringue, like sticky toffee inside, with a fresh fruit topping — a marvellous dinner party dessert.

3 egg whites
175 g (6 oz) soft light brown sugar
2 bananas, thinly sliced
300 ml (½ pint) double cream, whipped
15 ml (1 tablespoon) soft dark brown sugar
30 ml (2 tablespoons) rum (or 7.5 ml (1½ teaspoons) rum essence)
3 slices fresh pineapple, or 225 g (8 oz) canned pineapple chunks, drained

Heat the grill to Medium.

Whisk the egg whites until they are stiff enough to stand in peaks. Add the sugar gradually, whisking until the mixture holds its shape. Tip the mixture on to a piece of vegetable parchment paper on the baking dish and spread it out to about 4 cm (1½ in) deep. Using a knife or a spoon, build up the edge to make a slightly raised rim. Bake for about 20 minutes, or until the meringue is dry. Remove from the heat, cool, then peel off the backing paper.

Arrange the sliced bananas in the meringue case. Stir the dark brown sugar and the rum or essence into the cream and spread or pipe it over the fruit. Cut whole slices of pineapple into quarters. Decorate the top with a pattern of pineapple.

As an alternative
You can make an even gooier meringue with soft dark brown sugar. Don't worry if the meringue emerges sticky on the underside. That's part of its charm.

For a change
The above combination of fruits is hard to beat. But do try others. Canned apricots and peaches make a good topping too.
Serves 6

Appendix

List of Manufacturers

Breville Europe Ltd,
Alexander Terrace, Guildford, Surrey GUI 3DA

Kenwood: Thorn EMI Domestic Electrical Appliances Ltd.,
New Lane, Havant, Hampshire P09 2NH

Pifco Ltd,
Failsworth, Manchester M35 OHS

Sunbeam Electric Ltd,
Rutherford Road, Daneshill West, Basingstoke,
Hants RG24 0QY

Tefal UK Ltd,
11 – 49 Station Road, Langley, Slough, Berkshire SL3 8DR

Tower: T.I. Tower Housewares Ltd,
PO Box 16, Wolverhampton WV5 8AQ

Moulinex Ltd,
Station Approach, Coulsdon, Surrey CR3 2UD

Index

COOKING FOR GOOD HEALTH BOOKS NOW AVAILABLE IN GRANADA PAPERBACKS

Suzanne Beedell
Pick, Cook and Brew — £1.50 ☐

Ursula Gruniger
Cooking with Fruit — £1.50 ☐

Sheila Howarth
Grow, Freeze and Cook — £1.50 ☐

Kenneth Lo
Cooking and Eating the Chinese Way — £1.50 ☐
Chinese Cooking and Eating for Health — £1.25 ☐
The Wok Cookbook — £1.25 ☐

L D Michaels
The Complete Book of Pressure Cooking — £1.25 ☐

Miriam Polunin
The Right Way to Eat — £1.25 ☐

Franny Singer
The Slow Crock Cookbook — £1.50 ☐

Janet Walker
Vegetarian Cookery — £1.50 ☐

Beryl Wood
Let's Preserve It — 95p ☐

COOKERY HANDBOOKS NOW AVAILABLE IN GRANADA PAPERBACKS

Elizabeth Cass
Spanish Cooking   £1.25 ☐

Jean Graham
The Poldark Cookbook   £1.50 ☐

Ursula Gruniger
Cooking With Fruit   50p ☐

Marika Hanbury Tenison
Deep-Freeze Cookery   £1.95 ☐
New Fish Cookery   £1.25 ☐
West Country Cooking   £1.25 ☐
The Best of British Cooking   £1.50 ☐
Cooking with Vegetables   £1.95 ☐

Sheila Howarth
Grow, Freeze and Cook   £1.50 ☐

Robin Howe
Greek Cooking   £1.25 ☐
German Cooking   £1.50 ☐

Sheila Hutchins
Grannie's Kitchen
Recipes from the North of England   95p ☐
Recipes from East Anglia   95p ☐
Recipes from the West Country   £1.25 ☐

Kenneth Lo
Cooking and Eating the Chinese Way   £1.50 ☐
The Wok Cookbook   £1.25 ☐

Jennifer Stone
The Alcoholic Cookbook   £1.25 ☐

COOKERY HANDBOOKS NOW AVAILABLE IN GRANADA PAPERBACKS

L D Michaels
The Complete Book of Pressure Cooking   £1.95 ☐

F Marian McNeil
The Scots Kitchen   £1.95 ☐
The Scots Cellar   £1.95 ☐

Cecilia Norman
Pancakes & Pizzas   95p ☐
Micro-Wave Cookery Course   £1.50 ☐

Margaret Paterson
The Craft of Cooking   £1.50 ☐

David Scott
The Japanese Cookbook   £1.50 ☐

Franny Singer
The Slow Crock Cookbook   £1.50 ☐

E P Veerasawmy
Indian Cooking   £1.50 ☐

Janet Walker
Vegetarian Cookery   £1.50 ☐

Pamela Westland
Bean Feast   £1.50 ☐
The Everyday Gourmet   75p ☐
Food for Keeps   £1.95 ☐

Carol Wright
Complete Meat Cookery   £1.25 ☐

Arto Der Haroutunian
Complete Arab Cookery   £1.50 ☐

All these books are available at your local bookshop or newsagent, and can be ordered direct from the publisher.

To order direct from the publisher just tick the titles you want and fill in the form below:

Name _____

Address _____

_____

Send to:
Granada Cash Sales
PO Box 11, Falmouth, Cornwall TR10 9EN

Please enclose remittance to the value of the cover price plus:

UK 45p for the first book, 20p for the second book plus 14p per copy for each additional book ordered to a maximum charge of £1.63.

BFPO and Eire 45p for the first book, 20p for the second book plus 14p per copy for the next 7 books, thereafter 8p per book.

Overseas 75p for the first book and 21p for each additional book.